The Pale of Words

THE PALE OF WORDS

Reflections on the Humanities and Performance

JAMES ANDERSON WINN

Yale University Press   New Haven and London

Copyright © 1998 by Yale University.
All rights reserved.
This book may not be reproduced, in whole
or in part, including illustrations, in any form
(beyond that copying permitted by Sections 107 and 108
of the U.S. Copyright Law and except by reviewers
for the public press), without written permission
from the publishers.

Library of Congress Cataloging-in-Publication Data
Winn, James Anderson, 1947–
The pale of words : reflections on the humanities and performance /
James Anderson Winn.
p. cm.
Includes bibliographical references and index.
ISBN 0-300-07412-3 (acid-free paper)
1. Humanities—Study and teaching (Higher). 2. Learning and
scholarship. 3. Humanities—Philosophy. 4. Scholars. 5. Entertainers.
6. Literature—History and criticism—Theory, etc. I. Title.
AZ182.W56 1998   98-5743
001.3′071—dc21   CIP

Printed in the United States of America.

A catalogue record for this book is
available from the British Library.

The paper in this book meets the guidelines
for permanence and durability of the Committee
on Production Guidelines for Book Longevity of
the Council on Library Resources.

10 9 8 7 6 5 4 3 2 1

For Mara Jayne

Since Man from beast by Words is known,
Words are Man's province, Words we teach alone.

. . . .

Plac'd at the door of Learning, youth to guide,
We never suffer it to stand too wide.
To ask, to guess, to know, as they commence,
As Fancy opens the quick springs of Sense,
We ply the Memory, we load the brain,
Bind rebel Wit, and double chain on chain;
Confine the thought, to exercise the breath;
And keep them in the pale of Words till death.

—Alexander Pope, *The Dunciad,* IV, ll. 149-60

Contents

Preface

In October and November 1996, it was my privilege and pleasure to give the inaugural series of James Murray Brown lectures at the University of Aberdeen, made possible by a generous bequest and sponsored by the Department of English at that ancient university. George Rousseau, Regius Professor of English at Aberdeen and director of the Thomas Reid Institute, made many of the arrangements for my visit and provided a warm and well-equipped office for me at the institute. George Watson, head of the English Department, also took pains to assure the success of the lectures. In the series of concerts that took place during the same residency, my expert partners were Roger Williams, harpsichord and organ, the members of the Yggdrasil String Quartet, and the Aberdeen University Symphony Orchestra, conducted on this occasion by Dennis Assaf.

In reworking the lectures for publication, I have made relatively few alterations. The spoken versions addressed a general audience including undergraduates and members of the extramural community.as well as faculty and graduate students. Because I argue vigorously here that humanities scholars need to address a wider public, I have kept such an audience in mind in this version, perhaps most obviously in the basic exposition of theories in the third chapter. The exigencies of publication have unfortunately meant that the musical examples in the first chapter, played on tape in the lectures, appear here in score; in all but one case, however, the notes indicate where recordings may be found.

Although the argument here is substantially new, I have drawn from time to time on previous publications. Some of the material in chapter 1 is derived from *Unsuspected Eloquence: A History of the Relations between Poetry and Music* (Yale University Press, 1981), though the discussion here concerns only one strand of the many intertwined in that book. In chapter 2, I return to some passages quoted and analyzed in *"When Beauty Fires the Blood": Love and the Arts in the Age of Dryden* (Ann Arbor: University of Michigan Press, 1993), though again my interests here are somewhat different. Some parts of the discussion of the University of Michigan Institute for the Humanities in chapter 4 come from a collaborative essay, "The Intellectual Economy of Interdisciplinary Scholarship," coauthored with Fred L. Bookstein and published as *Institute for the Humanities Occasional Paper* no. 1 (1994).

Among those who read this work in draft, provided helpful suggestions, and asked searching questions let me name George Rousseau, Ian McLachlan, Tobin Siebers, Nicholas Delbanco, James G. Turner, and Robert D. Hume. Jim Blenko served as my research assistant and looked after my dog. My greatest debt, both personal and intellectual, is recorded in the dedication.

The Pale of Words

I

The Sirens' Song

I begin with a recent and extreme example of an ancient and stubborn prejudice, a passage from Allan Bloom's surprise best-seller, *The Closing of the American Mind* (1987):

> Picture a thirteen-year-old boy sitting in the living room of his family home doing his math assignment while wearing his Walkman headphones or watching MTV. He enjoys the liberties hard won over centuries by the alliance of philosophic genius and political heroism, consecrated by the blood of martyrs; he is provided with comfort and leisure by the most productive economy ever known to mankind; science has penetrated the secrets of nature in order to provide him with the marvelous, life-like electronic sound and image reproduction he is enjoying. And in what does progress culminate? A pubescent child whose body throbs with orgasmic rhythms; whose feelings are made articulate in hymns to the joys of onanism or the killing of parents; whose ambition is to win fame and wealth in imitating the drag-queen who makes the music. In short, life is made into a nonstop, commercially prepackaged masturbational fantasy.[1]

The virulence of this attack on rock music is astonishing—especially as the source is not a late-night fundamentalist radio preacher but a learned and urbane professor at the University of

Chicago, justly honored as a translator of Plato and Rousseau and an analyst of Shakespeare's politics. Considered in light of my subtitle, what Bloom says here looks like a case of the humanities *against* performance. He sets up a strong opposition between some values long associated with the humanities and some terrors long associated with performance, invoking on one hand "the alliance of philosophic genius and political heroism," deploring on the other those "hymns to the joys of onanism or the killing of parents."

Looked at from another angle, however, Professor Bloom's tirade is an instance of the humanities *as* performance. Far from being cool, rational, and cerebral, his vocabulary evokes the extreme imagery of religious and patriotic fervor in phrases like "the blood of martyrs" and employs the dismissive slang of homophobia in the sneering label "drag-queen." His rhetoric begins with a visual example—"Picture a thirteen-year-old boy"—then situates that boy within a partisan description of modern Western culture as a progress toward comfort and freedom. Next comes a stagy rhetorical question—"in what does progress culminate?"—and the answer to the question falls into clauses carefully organized to produce the effect of climax:

> A pubescent child
> > whose body throbs with orgasmic rhythms;
> > > whose feelings are made articulate
> > > > in hymns to the joys of onanism
> > > > or the killing of parents;
> > > whose ambition is to win fame and wealth
> > > > in imitating the drag-queen
> > > > who makes the music.

This is not the voice of dispassionate analysis or Socratic dialogue. The style is oral, rhythmic, hectoring. In its excess, it may even be somewhat self-parodic. It is, in short, a performance.

I do not share Professor Bloom's untroubled faith in our productive economy, marvelous science, and political happiness. Neither do I regard a performance by Madonna or Boy George as a threat to civilization. But I do admire the unabashed performative quality of Bloom's writing, even as I deplore its contents. In these reflections—historical in the first two chapters, theoretical in the third, pragmatic in the fourth—I contend that the modern disciplines called the humanities have identified themselves excessively with analytical processes based narrowly on language, thus disassociating themselves from performance in most of its guises. This drive to enclose the energies of past and present cultures within the confining covers of a book is historically false and pedagogically disastrous. Much of what humanists study originates in performance, and all good teaching ought to be alert to the living excitement of arts and ideas, eager to dramatize that excitement through fresh performative gestures.

At once the most abstract and the most emotionally powerful of the arts, music has been the flash point for some of the most extreme attacks on performance in Western history, many of them launched by people claiming to represent the humanities or humanism or human values. In this chapter, I want to consider some episodes in the history of the relations between words and music—sometimes intimate and productive, often competitive and strained—as a way of developing some ideas we may apply to other aspects of the larger question of humanities and performance. My story begins with the Sirens.

§

In the middle books of the *Odyssey*, the hero recounts his adventures to the hospitable and civilized Phaeacians, on whose shore he has been cast up naked and half-drowned, the only survivor of a shipwreck. An important character in his story is the enchantress Circe, who first turns some of his men into animals but then becomes his lover and advisor. She warns him about the Sirens,

> those creatures who spellbind any man alive,
> whoever comes their way. Whoever draws too close,
> off guard, and catches the Sirens' voices in the air—
> no sailing home for him, no wife rising to meet him.
> No happy children beaming up at their father's face.
> The high, thrilling song of the Sirens will transfix him,
> lolling there in their meadow, round them heaps of corpses,
> rotting away, rags of skin shriveling on their bones.[2]

Despite twenty-six intervening centuries and massive cultural differences, this passage has much in common with Bloom's warnings about the dangers of the Walkman. In both cases the seduction of music separates a male victim from his family: in Bloom's myth, electronic stimulation transports the boy from "the living room of his family home" to an artificial world of forbidden desires including "the killing of parents"; in Homer's, the sailor who listens becomes one of the shriveled carcasses on the beach, losing forever his imagined homecoming to his wife and "happy children."

The power of the Sirens comes from their "high, thrilling song." Homer's account says nothing about their physical appearance or their sexuality, but even without an explicit link, musical seduction surely suggests sexual seduction.[3] Circe, who has shared her bed with Odysseus, is also an enchantress and a singer; she knows he will want to hear the Sirens and suggests a plan:

                              Soften some beeswax
and stop your shipmates' ears, so none can hear,
none of the crew, but if *you* are bent on hearing,
have them tie you hand and foot in the swift ship,
erect at the mast-block, lashed by ropes to the mast
so you can hear the Sirens' song to your heart's content.
                              (12.47–52, p. 273)

This picture of the hero lashed to the mast, enjoying the song but prevented from acting on its temptation, may serve as a useful icon for the West's bad conscience about music. We want to hear the Sirens' song, but we fear that such pleasure can only lead to immorality and death, so we try to protect people we consider weaker or inferior—shipmates, students, children— from the power of music, whether by wax in their ears or electronic jamming of dangerous television channels.

There are terrible ironies in this story. In order to experience musical pleasure, the resourceful Odysseus, master of men and disguises, must allow himself to be bound like a slave or a criminal.[4] Pleasure requires giving up power. As in sexual fantasies of domination, powerful, frightening women are the source of forbidden delights, yet throughout the Western history of the arts, most women have been placed in the position of the deafened shipmates—forcibly protected from pleasures they are supposedly unable to resist. Men, including the men responsible for developing the practices of the modern humanities, have thus stigmatized performance as female and dangerous, while at the same time denying women access to performance or barring them from taking part in it.

At an even more basic level, it is surely a telling irony that this myth about the dangers of music comes to us in Greek epic poetry, a form whose origins were musical. Archaeologists and anthropologists agree that dancing, chanting, and the singing of meaningless syllables *preceded* the singing of actual words in prehistoric cultures; the first poets, long before the advent of written language, were those who learned how to add meaningful words to wordless songs and dances.[5] In Homeric verse, illustrated here by a musical transcription of the first two lines of the Sirens' song, long syllables are sustained, as they are in singing, and last twice as long as short syllables. The dominant pattern is a long syllable followed by two short ones, and the line always ends with two long syllables. Surely this kind of rhythm began as a dance; I always feel I can hear a drumbeat. There is also a kind of melody. Some of the vowels are sounded at a high pitch, some at a low pitch, and some with a slide up to and away from the high pitch. Those pitches, later indicated in written texts as accents, were a feature of all spoken ancient Greek, not just poetry, but in epic poetry, the combination of pitched syllables and dance rhythms is palpably musical.

In Homer's oral culture, hearing was more acute and mem-

ren   op'   a - kou - ses.

[Come closer, famous Odysseus—Achaea's pride and glory—
Moor your ship on our coast so you can hear our song!]⁶

ory more powerful than we can even imagine; his hearers were
closely attuned to the interplay of rhythm and pitch, which
gave each poetic line a distinct musical shape. In addition to the
rhythms and pitches charted in my transcription, they would
have heard the repetition of the *u* sound in *Deur', Oduseu,* and
kudos, as well as the chiming of syllables ending in the consonant *n*: *agion, poluain, Achaion.*⁷ The most common term for
such sound effects in poetry in any language is *assonance.* Literary critics also speak of vowel color, calling some vowels dark
and others bright. Linguists, locating the part of the mouth in
which we sound each vowel, speak of front vowels and back
vowels. But in acoustical physics, assonance is actually pitch.
There is a distinct overtone pitch for each vowel, produced by
the shaping of the speaker's mouth and throat. Poets of many
languages and periods have used the music of these pitches; if
you admire the way that Keats holds a line together by variation
and repetition of vowel sounds, you are admiring the melody
of his vowels. Even rhyme, considered in this way, is a melodic
device, promising a return to the same vowel, and thus to the
same overtone pitch, at the end of the line. So when poets argue
that music should be subservient to words, as they have often
done, they are denying not only the origins of poetry in music
but the continued importance of a musical ear in the making
of verse. Ezra Pound was closer to the truth when he gave his
own definition of poetry in 1918: "Poetry is a composition of
words set to music. Most other definitions of it are indefen-
sible, or metaphysical. . . . Poets who will not study music are
defective."⁸ Homer uses the word *aoidos,* which means singer,

to describe the bards who appear in his poem; he uses the same word to describe the Sirens.

We can make an even stronger claim for the musical origins of the other main kind of ancient Greek poetry, called *lyric* because it was invariably sung with an instrument, originally a lyre. Lyric poems included solo songs in honor of athletes or in praise of love, and choral songs danced and sung at religious festivals or in the tragic drama. The rhythms were much more complex than those of epic, often falling into patterns we might transcribe today as 5/8 or 7/8 time, and the melodies had more variety in pitch. The same person served as both poet and composer: Sappho and Pindar were as much admired for their music as for their words; Aristophanes contrasted the melodic styles of Aeschylus and Euripides. Unfortunately, virtually all of the melodies of these songs are lost to us; we have only a few scraps, all dating from the third century B.C. or later. Here is a partial reconstruction of one of the earliest fragments, a few lines from a chorus in Euripides' tragedy *Orestes*.

[I grieve, I grieve—your mother's blood that drives you wild. Great prosperity among mortals is not lasting: upsetting it like the sail of a swift sloop some higher power swamps it in the rough doom-waves of fearful toils, as of the sea.] [9]

It is hardly possible to draw sweeping generalizations from this isolated fragment. We do not even know whether these few notes are the music Euripides himself composed in the fifth century or a later version by someone else. But there can be no tion that music was of central importance in the composition of Greek lyric poetry. In a typical choral ode, the poet had to produce two sets of words to fit the same music. Even as late as Euripides, I suspect the music came first. A poet who invented the words for a stanza, or *strophe,* before composing the music would still have faced the task of making a second set of words, the *antistrophe,* to fit the same musical framework. At that moment, crafting words to conform to the rhythms and pitches of the first stanza, the poet was still a musician, but a potent force was already at work in the culture, pushing apart the once-unified arts of music and poetry. It was the alphabet.

§

The Greeks initially used the same word, *mousike,* to describe dance, music, poetry, and elementary education. Together with gymnastics, music was the basic form of learning. Boys and girls in seventh-century Sparta, for example, learned to perform choral songs that were supposed to make them loyal to the state and moral in their actions. [10] In the absence of writing, *mousike* was the best way to memorize and preserve the wisdom of the culture, and ancient Greeks trained in *mousike* had prodigious memories. Greek prisoners amazed their Sicilian captors by their ability to recall tragic choruses; many could also recite long stretches of the Homeric epics. [11] Patterns of rhythm and pitch evidently helped them retain both epic and lyric poetry in their minds. By representing the sounds of speech with graphic symbols, the alphabet preserved information in a completely different way. As a visual aid to memory, it was resisted by people who correctly believed it would weaken the oral and musical memories of their children, but like other technological innovations in more recent times, it inevitably triumphed. Ironically, many small children now learn the English alphabet by singing a song—a faint, vestigial survival of the old way of learning, with the added irony that the letters they are learning will soon enable them to dispense with such musical mnemonics.

As early as the fifth century, writing had joined music and gymnastics in Athenian primary education, and it soon became the most important subject.[12] This was a decisive moment in the history of the tension between the humanities and performance. Rather than memorize the Homeric poems, students could now write them down, and the resulting texts, abstracted away from performance, took on functions different from those served by the oral versions. Despite their origins in improvised, musical performance, the *Iliad* and the *Odyssey* were now physical objects, scrolls marked with symbols. The processes of editing, commentary, analysis, and criticism that we associate with the modern humanities began as soon as those poems became texts, and so, alas, did the disdain for performance that often characterizes modern scholarship. Virtually all Greek literature from prehistory until the death of Euripides was in poetry (and thus intimately connected to music); Plato and other philosophical writers during the next century used prose. This new division, with "creative" writing taking the form of poetry, "analytical" writing taking the form of prose, marks the beginning of what we might now call the separation of the disciplines. When the modern French theorist Roland Barthes, writing in 1980, speaks of "the uneasiness of being a subject torn between two languages, one expressive, the other critical,"[13] he is enacting once more the rift between performance and analysis originally produced by the introduction of the alphabet.

By the fourth century, the alphabet had also been pressed into service as a musical notation, with letters written above the vowels in a poetic line to indicate the pitch at which each syllable was to be sung. That innovation enables us to read the surviving scraps of ancient Greek music, including the one from Euripides, but the separation of poetic and musical notation—both using the alphabet, but written on different lines—confirms the growing separation between poetic and musical work. Reports of the dramatic festivals now began to include the names of virtuoso instrumentalists. A growing body of music theory, based on the work of the philosopher Pythagoras and elaborately mathematical in nature, explored some largely hypothetical problems in tuning and transposition. And a number of musicians and philosophers discussed the psychological and ethical effects of musical compositions based on various *harmoniai*. Sometimes referred to as a *mode*, a Greek *harmonia* has been usefully described as "a type of musical discourse: not only a particular disposition of the intervals but also specific pitch, modulation, color, intensity, and timbre, all the elements which distinguish the musical output of a particular geographical and cultural environment."[14] The names of the modes—Aeolian, Dorian, Lydian, Phrygian, and so forth—were the names of regions; Greek listeners recognized the differences as readily as you might recognize the differences between a Scottish folk song, a Beatles tune, and a Broadway show stopper. And just as parents and moralists in recent times have attempted to ban whole musical genres—ragtime, hot jazz, rock 'n roll, rap—there were ancient voices deploring some of the *harmoniai,* which allegedly encouraged various kinds of immoral behavior.

The most famous such critic was Plato, who banned all but two *harmoniai* from his utopian Republic. The fictionalized Socrates begins this part of the argument by announcing that "song consists of three elements: words, musical mode, and rhythm."[15] Significantly, the order in which he gives these elements *reverses* the order in which poetry developed: rhythm came first, then pitch, then finally words. As I have explained, Greek poets had to fit their words to music; they knew that the musical elements in their poetry would help future generations remember it. But Plato, who feared both music and writing, preferring the improvised immediacy of the spoken word,[16] could now argue that words were self-sufficient—"it will make no difference whether they are set to music or not"—and that they should dictate the character of any music used to set them—"the musical mode (the *harmonia*) and the rhythm should fit the words."

Plato's privileging of words over music continues to shape the typical practices of modern humanists. Let me draw some examples from a speech delivered in 1977 by A. Bartlett Giamatti, then president of Yale University. "I conceive of the humanities," says Giamatti, "as those areas of inquiry that are language- or, better, word-centered, and I conceive of the radical humanist activity, therefore, as revolving around the interpretation of a text."[17] But if the "radical humanist activity" is textual interpretation, drawing on the skills of the brain and the eye, what happens to the skills of tongue and ear, the dancing feet and chanting voices from which poetry was born? When Giamatti mentions the arts, he defines them as if they were all word-based, referring to "music theater, painting, sculpture, architecture, each with its own sign system or 'language,' and its own 'texts.'" Apparently unaware that the distorted view of the arts produced by describing them in this way contributes to their lack of prestige, he goes on to deplore the fact that "the arts are still viewed in many quarters, within the academy and without, as accidental, not essential, as ornamental, as something vaguely suspect, faintly interesting, and often useless" (143). We may trace these modern prejudices to the triumph of the alphabet and Plato's subsequent insistence on the self-sufficiency of language; unfortunately, the same forces have led well-meaning academic defenders of the arts to describe them in ways that deny them some essential parts of their power. I value music (and the other arts) precisely for those parts of their expressive and emotive force which are *unlike* language, *not* part of a sign system, not even easily *described* in language.

The air of moral superiority by which some later writers assert the primacy of words may also come from Plato. When Socrates asks which musical modes "express sorrow," his companion Glaukon, who is more knowledgeable about music, names "modes like the Mixed Lydian and Hyperlydian," which Socrates immediately discards, explaining that "men, and even women of good standing, will have no use for them" (3.398e; 86). The implicit sneer in the phrase about "women of good standing" underscores the misogynistic association of women with emotion, pleasure, and performance, apparent in the myth of the Sirens and still operative when Allan Bloom calls his exemplary rock performer a "drag-queen." The next sentence links "effeminacy" with "drunkenness and inactivity," pursuits that Socrates considers "most unsuitable" for the Guardians of his Republic, and pursuits associated with "the Ionian and certain Lydian modes which are called 'slack'" (3.398e; 86–87). By this process of elimination, Socrates reduces the permissible modes to the Dorian and the Phrygian, the oldest and most traditional *harmoniai*, the ones most comfortably associated with patriotism and virtue. And so, in the mythical Republic, the flowering of musical variety was to be cut off at the root.

Although poets from the Renaissance to our own time have sometimes joined in similar attempts to censor and limit music, the Greek poets fare no better than the musicians in the Republic. Socrates admires Homer and Hesiod but condemns them for "compos[ing] fictitious tales" and for sometimes making their stories "ugly and immoral as well as false" (2.377d–e; 69). Elsewhere, he speaks of the "inherent charm of metre, rhythm, and musical setting" (10.601a; 331) but goes on to assert that the poet cannot be admitted into the Republic "because he stimulates and strengthens an element which threatens to undermine the reason" (10.605b; 337). Again, there is a sharp contrast with earlier cultural practice, in which poetry was a medium for religious and civic instruction; the argument here is almost identical to the argument against those *harmoniai* associated with passionate and irrational behavior. If the kinds of poetry "directed to pleasure and imitation," now personified as female and plural, "have any argument to give showing that they should be in a city with good laws," says Socrates, "we should be delighted to receive them back from exile, since we are aware that we ourselves are charmed by them," but he has no intention of changing his mind because "it isn't holy to betray what seems to be the truth."[18] This looks like a philosophical version of Odysseus and the Sirens. By strenuous mental effort, Socrates resists both music and poetry, acknowledging their capacity to give pleasure and delight but banishing them nonetheless because of his belief that they are false or lying, while philosophy is true.

§

The advent of Christianity brought with it the potential for a different view of the relative value of words and music. In the Hebrew Synagogue, from which early Christian liturgical practice derived, singers chanted the Psalms (mainly on a single pitch) and warbled long, ecstatic melodies for the words *alleluia* and *amen*. Jewish and early Christian practice did not include dancing, regular meter, or instruments, but unaccompanied songs—the old Psalms and the new Christian hymns—were a central part of Christian worship. Christian Latin poets, including St. Augustine's teacher St. Ambrose, developed new poetic forms by fitting their words to tunes that probably originated in the Jewish liturgy. Here is an example of the resulting form.

Ae - ter - na Chris - ti mu - ne - ra   et mar - ty - rum vic - to - ri - as

Lau-des fe - ren-tes de - bi - tas,   lae - tis   ca - na-mus men - ti - bus.

[The eternal gifts of Christ and the victories of the martyrs
Bringing forth the praises we owe, we sing with happy minds.] [19]

The simple shape of these hymns, with short phrases neatly corresponding to the contours of the melody, suggests their devotional and didactic purpose; many converts record the importance of such music in helping them understand and embrace the new faith.

For Clement of Alexandria, writing in the second century A.D., Christ was not only the Word, the *logos* of John's Gospel, but the New Song. For Augustine, however, there was danger in music, even the music sung in church. "I was enthralled . . . by the pleasures of sound," he tells God in the *Confessions*, "but you broke my bonds and set me free." [20] In the myth of the Sirens, the bonds holding Odysseus to the mast were a physical representation of self-discipline, a restraint designed to prevent a fatal yielding to musical pleasure, but in Augustine's metaphor, the love of music is itself a kind of bondage, from which

God has freed him. Still, he worries about paying too much attention to the music in church:

> I admit that I still find some enjoyment in the music of hymns, which are alive with your praises, when I hear them sung by well-trained, melodious voices. But I do not enjoy it so much that I cannot tear myself away. I can leave it when I wish. But if I am not to turn a deaf ear to music, which is the setting for the words which give it life, I must allow it a position of some honour in my heart, and I find it difficult to assign it to its proper place. For sometimes I feel that I treat it with more honour than it deserves. (238–39)

The parenthetical claim that the words "give life" to the music is astonishing. It recalls but reverses St. Paul's famous comment on the Old Law: "The letter kills, but the spirit gives life" (2 Cor. 3.6). If Augustine had said that the music gave life to the words, we might think of the music as spirit, *pneuma*, the breath sustaining and bringing to life the dead letters of doctrine. But he says the opposite and thus outdoes even Plato in making music subservient to language. Acutely aware of his senses and alert to the power of music, Augustine struggles to suppress the slightest shiver of pleasure, but his desire to enlist the power of music in making converts almost overcomes his worry about gratifying the senses: "I am inclined to approve of the custom of singing in church, in order that by indulging the ears weaker spirits may be inspired with feelings of devotion" (239). Again, the reference to "weaker spirits" allows a comparison to the Homeric myth. Odysseus kept his weaker shipmates at their task by filling their ears with wax; Augustine allows the weaker spirits in his congregation to indulge their ears with music in the hope that they will be inspired to devotion.

The suspicion of music apparent in Augustine is even more overt in other medieval figures. Pope Gregory the Great, whose name we use to identify Gregorian chant, actually sought to suppress musical creativity by standardizing the liturgy. The emperor Charlemagne, progressive in so many other areas, embraced a similar program of musical censorship and uniformity by burning books containing Ambrosian chants. Despite such official attempts to control musical development and assert the primacy of the word, medieval music continued to gain complexity, and poets developed their art by fitting words to music. Liturgical chants became longer, more complex, and more ornate in the seventh and eighth centuries, and monkish singers, lacking a precise notation, found it especially hard to remember those parts of the repertory that were effectively wordless—the lengthy melodies sung to the last syllable of the word *alleluia*. In order to help his fellow singers remember the music, Notker Balbulus, a ninth-century monk, began writing new words for these passages; the resulting works, called *sequences,* decisively altered the shape of Latin poetry, moving it in the direction of modern stanzaic form.[21]

Like many other kinds of chant, sequences were sung antiphonally, with one choir responding to another. The next major development in musical technique, perhaps the single most stunning advance in the history of Western music, was *polyphony,* in which two or more musical lines were sung simultaneously. We are so accustomed to multivoiced music that we need to remember that it was once new, and to consider for a moment its decisive impact on the relations between words and music. As soon as there is more than one part, it becomes much more difficult to hear the words, especially if different parts are singing different words, as in this example from the thirteenth-century *Worcester Fragments*.[22]

cre - a - to - ris, Do - mi - na cle - men - ti - ae.

om - ni - um, Sy -

Spi - ran - tis sa - cra - ri - um

qui coe - lum

[Choir: Hail, holy Mother, who labored to bear the King Who rules heaven and earth . . .

Tenor 1:

Hail, Mother of the Redeemer,
fountain of mercy,
vessel of honor,
flower of comeliness,
palace of the King of glory,
bride of heaven's Creator,
lady of clemency . . .

Tenor 2:

Hail light of the suffering,
comforter of mankind,
flower and ornament of virgins,
bearer of the Son of God,
King of all kings,
Star in the darkness, . . .

Tenor 3:

Hail, rose without thorn
purple flower,
medicine to the sick
stream from a sweet fountain,
shrine of the living God, . . .]23

Here there is at least some theological simultaneity: the phrases the various parts are singing are all metaphors for the Virgin Mary. In some later medieval motets, however, different voices sing in different languages. In one remarkable example, a motet with a Latin text in praise of St. Catherine includes an upper part with an obscene Provençal text celebrating the love of the flesh.[24] As in other forms of medieval art, the spirit and the flesh are not engaged in a dialectic here but envisioned as higher and lower versions of the same thing, yet in practical terms, it must have been impossible to attend to both texts simultaneously. Homer had envisioned only two Sirens, singing in unison; Isidore of Seville, writing in the seventh century, specified three Sirens—one singing, one playing a wind instrument, and one playing the lyre.[25] The late medieval heirs of Plato and Augustine, still desperately asserting the primacy of language, now faced a whole choir of Sirens, singing counterpoint in different melodies and languages. No wonder visual representations from this period show the Sirens with wings and fishtails, making them monsters.

§

Like other innovations, polyphony was quickly tamed; composers soon learned how to make the text more audible by putting it in the highest voice and treating the lower parts as accompaniment. When the first generation of Renaissance scholars promoted a new rereading of the ancient poets and rhetoricians, with fresh interest in persuasion, emotion, and the moral force of sounds, musicians responded to the challenge. Medieval composers had often worked out their music before pasting in a text, but Renaissance composers normally started with a text and worked in various ways at animating or expressing it. Josquin des Pres, the greatest composer of the early sixteenth century, used dissonant harmonies at painful moments in the text; when his contemporaries wished to praise him, they compared him to Virgil, who was justly famous for making the sounds of his poetic Latin appropriate to the subject matter. Josquin's innovations pointed the way toward the rhetorical musical expression of the Italian madrigal school, which developed a number of harmonic and melodic conventions for setting particular words. Soon every trained composer knew a large vocabulary of musical equivalents for words expressing speed or slowness, climbing or falling, height or depth, and various modes of motion. Many of these are obvious—a leap to a high note on the word "high" or "sky," a descent for "low" or "grave"; others are only a little more metaphorical, like a circular melody for the word "round" or a falling half-step for "dying," which became more or less required in both madrigal and opera. This vocabulary of stock devices, sometimes called *madrigalisms,* was one important version of imitation for

Renaissance and baroque composers. Although somewhat belated, the funniest English illustration of these techniques is a mock-cantata by Jonathan Swift, into which the author has crammed every possible stock phrase requiring a conventional text-setting device, thus:

> For Pegasus runs every Race
> By Galloping high, or Level Pace,
> Or Ambling or Sweet Canterbury,
> Or with a high down derry,
> No Victory he ever got,
> By Jogling, Jogling, Jogling trot.
> No Muse harmonious Entertains,
> Rough Roystring Rustick Roaring Strains
> Nor shall you twine the Crackling Bays
> By Sneaking Sniv'ling Round Delays.

The composer, John Echlin, responded deftly.[26]

No Muse har-mon-ious En-ter-tains, Rough Royst---ring Rus---tick Roar---ing Strains nor shall you twine---the Crack---ling, Crack-ling Bays by Sneak---ing Sniv'l---ling Round---De---lays.

This cantata is meant to illustrate the limitations of "word-painting," its tendency to make both words and music degenerate into nonsense. Swift wrote it during the 1720s, but the criticisms of madrigalism he dramatizes had already been made in Italy as early as the 1590s, by a group of intellectual aristocrats called the Musical Humanists. Although they wanted music to serve and express the text, the Musical Humanists opposed directly imitative word-painting. Most of them also opposed complex musical rhythms, arguing that music should exactly follow the rhythm of the poem. They deplored the staggered declamation typical of the madrigal, with different voices singing different words at the same time, preferring simpler choral singing in block chords or lightly accompanied solo singing—techniques that made the words easier to hear. Some of them went so far as to propose banning all harmony, advocating a strictly syllabic declamation of the text by a solo voice. At first blush, these reformers look less hostile to music and emotion than Plato or Augustine. They allude frequently and admiringly to ancient tales of the power of music in Greek tragedy. But their own resistance to music becomes apparent when they conclude that it will best arouse the passions by submitting to the rule of the text: their legacy is the operatic recitative, in which the words essentially control the music. Fortunately for the history of music, their project was hijacked by Claudio Monteverdi, a shrewd and subtle reader of poetry, but a composer unwilling to let the humanist reform program deprive his art of the full range of musical technique it had developed since the Middle Ages.[27]

Some of the richest English poems drawing on the myth of the Sirens come from this period of ferment and controversy. In one of the best-known episodes in Spenser's *Faerie Queene*, for example, Sir Guyon visits the Bower of Bliss, home of the enchantress Acrasia, where he is tempted by two "naked Damzelles" in a fountain:

> Sometimes the one would lift the other quight
> Above the waters, and then downe againe
> Her plong, as over maistered by might,
> Where both awhile would covered remaine,
> And each the other from to rise restraine;

> The whiles their snowy limbes, as through a vele,
> So through the Christall waves appeared plaine:
> Then suddeinly both would themselves unhele,
> And th' amarous sweet spoiles to greedy eyes revele.
>
> .   .   .   .
>
> Whom such when *Guyon* saw, he drew him neare,
> And somewhat gan relent his earnest pace,
> His stubborne brest gan secret pleasaunce to embrace.[28]

Here the temptation is visual and fleshly, and it takes a timely intervention by his faithful Palmer to keep Guyon from yielding, but no sooner have they got past the two damsels than temptation reappears in the form of explicitly polyphonic music:

> Eftsoones they heard a most melodious sound,
> Of all that mote delight a daintie eare,
> Such as attonce might not on living ground,
> Save in this Paradise, be heard elswhere:
> Right hard it was, for wight, which did it heare,
> To read, what manner musicke that mote bee:
> For all that pleasing is to living eare,
> Was there consorted in one harmonee,
> Birdes, voyces, instruments, windes, waters, all agree.
>
> (2.12.70)

When Spenser tells us that it was "Right hard . . . for wight, which did it heare,/To *read,* what manner musicke that mote be," his choice of words reflects the conditions of reading in the Renaissance. An educated person might read Spenser's poem and might also be able to read his or her part in a madrigal sung after dinner. But when listening to a whole polyphonic piece, with all the parts "consorted in one harmonee," a hearer would find it difficult to "read" the meaning of the overlapping contrapuntal voices. What is difficult becomes dangerous; what the poet cannot read, he associates with sin.

The last line of this stanza lists five parts—"Birdes, voyces, instruments, windes, waters"—and the next stanza is a poetic attempt to suggest the polyphony of those parts.

> The joyous birdes shrouded in chearefull shade,
> Their notes unto the voyce attempred sweet;
> Th' Angelicall soft trembling voyces made
> To th' instruments divine respondence meet:
> The silver sounding instruments did meet
> With the base murmure of the waters fall:
> The waters fall with difference discreet,
> Now soft, now loud, unto the wind did call:
> The gentle warbling wind low answered to all.
>
> (2.12.71)

Technically impressive as poetry, this stanza is a doomed attempt to provide a verbal equivalent for the actual complexity of polyphonic music. What Spenser faintly suggests by repetition and overlap, polyphonic music accomplishes by simple simultaneity. Some of the hostility toward music expressed by Renaissance poets must stem from the recognition that polyphony gave composers expressive resources for which there were no poetic equivalents. Outdone by their rivals, the poets fell back on the ancient and Christian traditions associating music with the temptations of the flesh.

The music in the Bower of Bliss may sound "Angelicall" and "divine," but it is another temptation, as Guyon and the Palmer soon discover:

> There, whence that Musick seemed heard to bee,
> Was the faire Witch her selfe now solacing,
> With a new Lover, whom through sorceree

And witchcraft, she from farre did thither bring:
There she had him now layd a slombering
In secret shade, after long wanton joyes:
Whilst round about them pleasauntly did sing
Many faire Ladies, and lascivious boyes,
That ever mixt their song with light licentious toyes.

(2.12.72)

Taken as a whole, the episode separates and elaborates the elements of the myth of the Sirens: first the fleshly temptation of the naked damsels; then the magical music of birds, voices, instruments, water, and winds; and finally the combination, as the "light licentious" music of the "faire Ladies and lascivious boyes" accompanies Acrasia's amours with her new lover. The music, as in the original myth, is virtually equivalent to the "sorceree/And witchcraft" by which she has brought the unfortunate knight to her bower.

Writing some forty years later, John Milton refers to poetry and music as a "Blest pair of Sirens" in his early poem "At a Solemn Music." At first blush, he appears to be assimilating the pagan myth of seduction and death into a safe Christian context, and his biography suggests some reasons he might have been less hostile toward music than Spenser: Milton's father was a composer, he himself played daily on the organ, and during his early trip to Italy, he visited with the Musical Humanists. Yet in christianizing such pagan figures as the Sirens and the Muses, Milton reveals his own unease about the power of music:

Blest pair of Sirens, pledges of Heav'n's joy,
Sphere-born harmonious Sisters, Voice and Verse,
Wed your divine sounds, and mixt power employ
Dead things with inbreath'd sense able to pierce,
And to our high-rais'd fantasy present

> That undisturbed Song of pure concent,
> Aye sung before the sapphire-color'd throne
> To him that sits thereon,
> With Saintly shout and solemn Jubilee.[29]

Milton asks "Voice and Verse," music and poetry, to bring their powers together in order to allow us to hear the "undisturbed Song of pure concent," but his choice of words disturbs that unfallen song with the troubling impurities of pagan myth. When he calls the sister arts "pledges of Heaven's joy," he invokes a meaning of the word *pledge* common in the Renaissance: "applied to a child, as a token or evidence of mutual love and duty between parents,"[30] a sense frequently used in love poems describing children, or future children, as the pledges of the earthly delights of fleshly lovers. But who, in this poem, are the parents of "Voice and Verse"? If the sisters are angels, they must be the children of the Christian God, but the mythic pattern that actually drives this passage is the pagan idea of the Muses as daughters born from the sexual union of Zeus and Mnemosyne, the goddess of Memory. As in the opening reference to a "Blest pair of Sirens," a pagan myth, erotic in nature, lurks behind a Christian one. When the poet asks "Voice and Verse" to "*wed* [their] divine sounds" his imperative verb seems an odd one to use in addressing two female figures; in the next line, the combined power of voice and verse is "able to *pierce*"—a curiously male verb. If Voice and Verse are nominally sisters, their "power" is nonetheless "mixt," combining male and female, pagan and Christian. The dissonances created by yoking these contrasting elements may suggest Milton's sense of the difficulties and dangers inherent in yoking music and poetry.

In Milton's scheme, the "mixt power" of the two arts is potent, able to resurrect dead things and help us hear the music of the spheres, to which we can return when one with God.

But in describing the music of the "celestial consort," the poet manages to award the primacy to words. Though accompanied by trumpets and harps, the heavenly music has texts; the choir sings "Hymns devout and holy Psalms," two kinds of music approved by the English Puritans, and two kinds in which the text precedes the musical setting. Ostensibly urging the union of "Voice and Verse," this poem enacts once more the desire of philosophers, poets, and preachers to control music. Renaissance poets often slyly equated the fallen aspects of music with developments in musical style that tended to obscure poetic meaning or form, and Milton's account of the Fall as a loss of harmony echoes the charges leveled against musical innovations by the Musical Humanists: disproportion, jarring discord, harsh sounds:

> disproportion'd sin
> Jarr'd against nature's chime, and with harsh din
> Broke the fair music that all creatures made
> To their great Lord, whose love their motion sway'd
> In perfect Diapason, whilst they stood
> In first obedience and their state of good.

The image of concord as obedience is another version of control; any desire for kinds of musical expression stretching beyond the "perfect Diapason" (an orderly scale) is not only din but sin. In this Christian recasting of the primal myth of the Sirens, music again enacts temptation.

As we have already seen in Spenser's poetic imitation of polyphony, Renaissance poets also used poems concerned with music as opportunities to display their own formal virtuosity, the music inherent in their poetry, thus implying that music was actually unnecessary. Such techniques can be imitative, as in the metrical inversions that place an accented syllable at the start of the line, imitating the violence of the verbs:

> Jarr'd against nature . . .
> Broke the fair music . . .

Less obvious but no less important are large-scale structures, formal proportions in which the poet imitates musical forms. Milton's syntactical skill allows him to spin one sentence for twenty-four of this poem's twenty-eight lines, perhaps an imitation of music's own capacity for unbroken, sustained development. Although short enough to be a candidate for musical treatment, this poem was never set to music. Perhaps Henry Lawes, who collaborated with Milton on the songs in *Comus*, recognized that the poet had built so much musical meaning into the words themselves that a setting might seem redundant.

In the last decade of the seventeenth century, John Dryden collaborated with Henry Purcell to produce a semiopera called *King Arthur.* Combining sexuality and singing, the elements Spenser had developed in sequence, Dryden wrote a scene in which two naked damsels in a pool, called "Syrens" in the stage directions, tempt the hero with their music and their bodies:

> *Come Bathe with us an Hour or two,*
> *Come Naked in, for we are so;*
> *What Danger from a Naked Foe?*
> *Come Bathe with us, come Bathe and share,*
> *What Pleasures in the Floods appear;*
> *We'll beat the Waters till they bound*
> *And Circle round, around, around,*
> > *And Circle round, around.*
> > > (Act IV, p. 37)[31]

Here is part of Purcell's ravishing setting.[32]

Purcell respects the natural accent of English words and the flow of the poetic phrase, but some of his finest effects come in moments that hesitate, repeat phrases, and even alter the text. Where Dryden had written, "Come Bathe with us an Hour or two," with the stress falling on "Bathe," Purcell places the important and explicitly sexual verb "Come" in a much more prominent position by accenting and repeating it four times, with an enticing series of overlapping slurs. He also repeats the ironic phrase "What danger from a naked foe," with shocking dissonances between the voices to signal the real danger of the temptation. Dryden should have recognized these changes as improvements, but he complains in his preface that "the Numbers of Poetry and Vocal Musick, are sometimes so contrary, that in many places I have been oblig'd to cramp my Verses, and make them rugged to the Reader, that they may be harmonious to the Hearer" (sig. A4v). Again a poet resists the musical rhythm a composer wants to impose on the text—a position much like that taken by the Musical Humanists one hundred years earlier.

In his preface to *Albion and Albanius,* a completely sung opera performed in 1685, Dryden is even grumpier:

> The nature of an *Opera* denies the frequent use of
> . . . poetical Ornaments: for Vocal Musick, though
> it often admits a loftiness of sound: yet always ex-
> acts an harmonious sweetness; or to distinguish yet
> more justly, The recitative part of the *Opera* requires
> a more masculine Beauty of expression and sound:
> the other, which (for want of a proper *English*
> Word) I must call *The Songish Part*, must abound
> in the softness and variety of Numbers: its princi-
> pal Intention, being to please the Hearing, rather
> than to gratify the understanding. (*Works,* XV, 3–4)

In criticism as in the plots of his plays, Dryden draws upon the ideology of gender, praising the recitative for its "masculine Beauty of expression and sound," leaving us to infer that "the other," *"The Songish Part"* with its "softness and variety," is feminine. The allegedly masculine recitative is the most literary part of any opera, the part in which music is most dominated by words. Dryden's fear of forms more strongly shaped by musical considerations, in which the text is obscured by polyphonic complexity or overwhelmed by melodic beauty, may remind us of the psychological forces driving misogyny itself. Conscious of the appeal of "softness and variety," of the delight that can come from an art aimed frankly at pleasing, men in Dryden's period (and later) uneasily resorted to claims of superior rationality and warned against the seductive power of beauty. The close association between music and water in the myth of the Sirens aids this process: by describing music as a liquid element, Dryden and other writers deny its structure, its architecture, its status as a made thing; instead, they make it seem fluid, formless, and dangerous.

§

The triumph of pure instrumental music in the late eighteenth century should have discredited this view forever. When Londoners crowded into concert halls to hear symphonies by Haydn during the 1790s, they were effectively disproving the view that the purpose of music was to animate or express a text. Although it took theory some years to adjust to practice, the emergence of a self-sufficient instrumental music destroyed not only the notion of music's subservience to words, but also the related idea that its function was imitative or mimetic.[33] Romantic thinkers, especially in Germany, enthusiastically embraced the notion of music as "the art most immediately expressive of spirit and emotion."[34] Yet even those intellectuals who abandoned verbal and mimetic criteria found ways to discredit music. Kant's judgment is all too typical:

> Although it speaks by means of mere sensations without concepts, and so does not, like poetry, leave anything over for reflection, [music] yet moves the temperament in a greater variety of ways and more intensely, although only transitorily. It is, however, rather enjoyment than cultivation . . . and in the judgment of reason it has less worth than any other of the beautiful arts.[35]

Unfortunately for music and the other performing arts, these ideas retain considerable power in the modern university. Musically illiterate and thus unable to grasp the concepts by which music actually speaks, professors of literature, philosophy, and history often fall back on the notion that music communicates entirely by sensation and appeals exclusively to emotion. In embracing such a reductive and limited view, they are the heirs not only of Kant, but of Augustine and Plato, unwitting allies of kinds of political and religious oppression they would normally be eager to deplore.

Many poets have also continued to resist the power of music, associating it with dark, irrational forces. Lawrence Binyon, in 1925, described the Sirens as "fond perfidious Voices" who "hunger to entice us/Beyond the borders of knowledge," as if it were not precisely the function of art in all its forms to transport us beyond those borders.[36] In Binyon's unwillingness to credit kinds of knowledge and experience other than the verbal, we encounter once more the stubborn prejudice enacted in the original myth.

A fortunate exception, a poem pointing in the right direction, is W. H. Auden's sonnet entitled "The Composer":

All the others translate: the painter sketches
A visible world to love or reject;
Rummaging into his living, the poet fetches
The images out that hurt and connect,

From Life to Art by painstaking adaption,
Relying on us to cover the rift;
Only your notes are pure contraption,
Only your song is an absolute gift.

Pour out your presence, a delight cascading
The falls of the knee and the weirs of the spine,
Our climate of silence and doubt invading;

You alone, alone, imaginary song,
Are unable to say an existence is wrong,
And pour out your forgiveness like a wine.[37]

Auden celebrates music as "pure contraption," free from the
burdens of imitation, blessedly unable to pass judgment. The
delight it gives cascades as liquid through the body of the
hearer, imagined as a landscape like the island of the Sirens.
Where the sterner voices we have sampled feared that musical pleasure would lead to drowning, improper emotions, sexual
sin, or the loss of rationality, Auden pictures it pouring out forgiveness like sacramental wine. His view is truly humane.

II

"Vain Shows"

In 1681, John Dryden published a play called *The Spanish Fryar*, which had been a considerable success in the theatre a few months earlier. In his preface, he took pains to make a distinction between the experience of reading the play and the experience of seeing it acted. "A judicious Reader," he predicted, "will discover in his Closet that trashy stuff, whose glittering deceiv'd him in the action."

> In a Play-house, everything contributes to impose upon the Judgment: the Lights, the Scenes, the Habits, and above all, the Grace of Action, which is commonly the best where there is the most need of it, surprise the Audience, and cast a mist upon their Understandings; not unlike the cunning of a Juggler, who is always staring us in the face, and overwhelming us with gibberish, only that he may gain the opportunity of making the cleaner conveyance of his Trick[.] But these false Beauties of the Stage are no more lasting than a Rainbow; when the Actor ceases to shine upon them, when he gilds them no longer with his reflection, they vanish in a twinkling. . . . But as 'tis my interest to please my Audience, so 'tis my Ambition to be read; that I am sure is the more lasting and the nobler Design: for the propriety of thoughts and words, which are the hidden beauties of a Play, are but confus'dly judg'd in the vehemence of Action. (sig. A2r–A3r)

Dryden's plays made use of all the illusionistic resources of the Restoration playhouse—wing-and-drop scenery, elaborate costumes, stylized acting. But his imagery here denies life and substance to the visual components of the performance, which he calls confusing mists and vanishing rainbows. The actor, already demeaned by the comparison to the cheating juggler, participates in this optical imagery when Dryden says that he *shines* upon the "false Beauties of the Stage," "*gild[ing]* them . . . with his *reflection*."

The basis for this downgrading of performance becomes clear when Dryden declares that his "Ambition to be *read* . . . is the more lasting and the nobler Design." Acknowledging that his "thoughts and words . . . are the *hidden* beauties of a Play," he nonetheless insists that these hidden beauties will last by virtue of being reduced to a printed text, while all other aspects of the performance will vanish. Like many other writers, Dryden is afraid that the emotional response viewers may have to performance will compromise their intellectual and moral capacity. We catch that fear in his verbs: the performance *deceives* us, *imposes* upon our judgment, "*surprise[s] us, . . . cast[s]* a mist upon [our] Understandings," and *overwhelm[s]* us like the juggler. Suspicious of these irrational responses, Dryden prefers to address "a judicious Reader . . . in his Closet," whose rational judgment of "the propriety of thoughts and words" will be unaffected by the confusion and vehemence of an actual performance.

This passage is a poignant instance of the way playwrights in many eras and cultures have tried to separate their enterprise from the work of the actor, the set designer, and the costume maker. Of course Dryden needed these collaborators and wanted a successful performance, as he indicates by conceding that it is in his "interest" to please the audience, but "interest" represents the present and the need for money, while "Ambition" represents the future and the need for a lasting reputation. Still, if Dryden's sole "Ambition [was] to be read," we might reasonably ask why he wrote drama at all, and there is surely an element of self-criticism in this passage. Elsewhere in the same preface, remembering some excessive rant he had written for his earlier stage heroes, Dryden makes that element explicit: "All I can say for those passages, which are I hope not many, is, that I knew they were bad enough to please, even when I writ them: But I repent of them amongst my sins" (sig. A2v).

Like the poets and philosophers we considered in chapter 1, with their various strategies for insisting on the subordination of music to words, playwrights have often liked to pretend that their words are the essence of the drama, and in practice, modern scholars often accept that false assumption. Every teacher who treats a modern paperback text of *Hamlet* as if it were *Hamlet* is a participant in this reductive distortion. Before we sneer at Dryden for dismissing many of the devices that contributed to the success of his plays, we should recognize that we often place our students in the position of the "judicious Reader . . . in his Closet." When we ignore the visual, gestural, vocal, scenic, and rhythmic parts of a play, we falsify the experience of drama. A play reduced to its words is missing at least as many of its dimensions as a symphony reduced to its score.

And the missing dimensions are those which set the drama apart from other kinds of literature. The Greek word from which *theatre* is derived, *theatron,* means "a place for seeing," and the wonderfully literal English term *show* converts a verb of visual display into a noun. In the American South of my childhood, the cinema was more simply called "the picture show," and the theatre is always and in essence a visual, sensory experience. Antonin Artaud, oracular prophet of the modern theatre, has given powerful expression to this view. "The stage," he says, "is a concrete physical place which asks to be filled, and to be given its own concrete language to speak. . . . This concrete language, intended for the senses and independent of speech, has first to satisfy the senses; . . . there is a poetry of the senses as there is a poetry of language, and . . . this concrete physical language . . . is truly theatrical only to the degree that the thoughts it expresses are beyond the reach of the spoken language."[1] The contrast with Dryden could hardly be more complete, as Artaud locates the essence of theatre in precisely those concrete, physical, visual processes that Dryden dismisses as misleading. Artaud's passionate intensity suggests the power of the forces arrayed against his view, as does the fact that he chooses to describe the nonverbal means of expression he is emphasizing as "a concrete language." Perhaps he believed that he could only gain respect for "music, dance, plastic art, pantomime, mimicry, gesticulation, intonation, architecture, lighting, and scenery" (39) by claiming that they were kinds of language—indeed, kinds of poetry.

Like the prejudice against music, the prejudice against theatrical spectacle has a long history, running from Plato to the Puritans, from Rousseau to the modern university. Although I cannot tell the whole story here, I want to select some episodes that illustrate three main kinds of prejudice, each of which we have already noticed in Dryden: (1) distrust of spectacle as illusory, (2) disdain for spectacle as ephemeral, and (3) fear of spectacle for its capacity to move us emotionally. These have been persistent strains in Western thought, with different versions dominating in different periods. Not least among their unfortunate results is an increasing distance between teachers of the humanities, who tend to be devotees of the written word, and our students, who respond more immediately and powerfully to visual images, especially the moving, dramatized images of the cinema and the television.

§

Ancient theatre, with its dancing, singing choruses, its masked and elaborately costumed actors, its stylized forms and gestures, was certainly closer to Artaud's vision than to Dryden's. Yet doubts about theatrical show appear as early as Plato's *Republic,* which includes a blistering critique of the theatre written by a man privileged to see some of the great works of Greek tragedy in their first performances. Plato does not develop the second of our three points, the ephemeral nature of theatrical effects, presumably because his larger theory of ideal Forms led him to see all earthly things as temporary. But his discussion is the original instance of the other two kinds of criticism, directly linking visual illusion to moral corruption. Socrates starts this section innocently enough, pointing out the limits of our sight. "An object seen at a distance," he explains, "does not . . . look the same size as when it is close at hand; a straight stick looks bent when part of it is under water; and the same thing appears concave or convex to an eye misled by colours. Every sort of confusion like these is to be found in our minds, and it is this weakness in our nature that is exploited, with a quite magical effect, by many tricks of illusion, like scene-painting and conjuring" (10.602c-d; 334). Within two sentences, the discussion slides from the ordinary limits of our sight when observing nature to the deliberate trickery of "scene-painting and conjuring," the same elements linked by Dryden some two thousand years later. In referring to scene-painting, Plato attacks a recent theatrical innovation: Sophocles, who was still active during the first twenty years of Plato's life, was the first Greek dramatist to use painted scenes. In referring to conjuring, Plato emphasizes the fact that our eyes can be fooled by clever technique and links performances we think of as high art (like the plays of Sophocles) to the vulgar feats of street magicians.

As these allusions to performance suggest, this is not a dispassionate analysis of the limits of human sight. By beginning his attack on dramatic poetry in the *Republic* with examples of optical illusion, Plato appears to treat the drama, an art including words, as if it were entirely an art of spectacle. The pivot on which his argument turns is the word *mimesis,* which is normally translated as "imitation." Recent scholarship, however, has revealed that the word originally meant "enactment," "impersonation," or "performance." The root is the word *mimos,* from which we derive our English *mime;* it originally meant "an actor in a cult drama." Eva Keuls, who has studied all the occurrences of both words before Plato, concludes that "the central notion in most passages is . . . *the conveyance of meaning through gestures of mimicry, rhythmic or otherwise."* [2] The long history of mimetic theories of the arts would have been very different if gesture and rhythm had maintained their central place in the idea of mimesis. Western theorists have unfortunately taken a much more limited view, treating mimesis as mere imitation and frequently employing such visual analogies as the mirror. Both kinds of narrowing stem from the very discussion in the *Republic* that we are considering, in which Plato stacks the deck against performance by using painting as his central example of mimesis, thus shrinking this vital term to make it mean something like "copying."

Most ancient paintings, like most ancient plays, were depictions of historical and mythical figures; like the tragedies, paintings retold familiar stories in a representational mode. Yet sources more friendly to the visual than Plato make it clear that the greatest Greek painters were admired for more than verisimilitude; the best of them were said to be able to capture the personalities of those they painted and move the emotions of those who saw the painting. By defining *mimesis* as mere imitation, Plato ignores such claims, just as he suppresses the rhythmic and gestural aspects of dramatic mimesis. Instead, he insists on judging painting (and thus drama) by "the standard of truth and reality." By that standard, even the most astonishingly lifelike paintings will inevitably be found wanting because they reduce three-dimensional reality to a single surface. By flattening out and misrepresenting both arts, Plato can use the limits of figurative painting as a basis on which to criticize both arts for a lack of realism and truth. And this is precisely the argument Socrates now offers, arguing that "paintings and works of art in general are far removed from reality," while "the element in our nature which is accessible to art and responds to its advances is equally far from wisdom" (603b; 334–35). By a conjuring trick of his own, Plato has equated the physical "weakness in our nature" that is "exploited" by optical illusions with an alleged weakness in our emotional and moral nature that "responds to [the] advances" of art—so that art becomes a seducer, and the viewer of art or drama becomes his prey. The playwright is "the counterpart of the painter, whom he resembles in two ways: his creations are poor things by the standard of truth and reality, and his appeal is not to the highest part of the soul, but to one which is equally inferior" (605b; 336–37). Therefore, declares Socrates with an air of triumph, "dramatic poetry has a most formidable power of corrupting even men of high character" (605c; 337).

Plato's main purpose in urging a narrow definition of *mimesis* is to gain a position from which to indict the theatre for its moral effects, and here the discussion has more to do with character and psychology than with visual display. Warming to his task, Socrates indicts both epic poetry and tragic drama for inducing in us the feelings displayed by the characters:

When we listen to some hero in Homer or on the tragic stage moaning over his sorrows in a long tirade, or to a chorus beating their breasts as they chant a lament, you know how the best of us enjoy giving ourselves up to follow the performance with eager sympathy. The more a poet can move our feelings in this way, the better we think him. And yet when the sorrow is our own, we pride ourselves on being able to bear it quietly like a man, condemning the behaviour we admired in the theatre as womanish. . . . To enter another's feelings must have an effect on our own: the emotions of pity our sympathy has strengthened will not be easy to restrain when we are suffering ourselves. (605c–606b; 337–38)

Greek attitudes toward gender and sexuality were quite unlike our own, so it is difficult to know exactly what Plato means by referring to theatrical displays of emotion as "womanish." There were no real women on the Greek stage; the actors playing Clytemnestra or Jocasta were female impersonators. Women were allowed to attend the tragic festivals but seated in the upper rows, far away from the action, as if too close a confrontation with the passions displayed were more dangerous for them than for male spectators. The cult of homosexual affection for beautiful boys, celebrated in a number of Plato's other dialogues, doubtless also had some effect on how the audience understood the jealousies, fears, and sorrows enacted in the plays. But even if we cannot perfectly recover the particular attitudes of this or any other society, we may surely identify the fear of sexual transgression or ambiguity as one of the most urgent components of the fear of theatrical emotion. We have already noticed a number of misogynistic gestures in passages expressing the fear of music, so it should not surprise us to en-counter misogyny in this and later expressions of disdain for the visual. As Iris Murdoch has remarked, Plato's opinions often make it possible to speak of him as a Puritan,[3] and we can find links running from Plato to the English Puritans, who closed the theatres as soon as they seized power, all the way to the self-appointed guardians of modern society, who argue that violent or sexy movies weaken the character of those who watch them.

Narrowly construed, Plato's attack on all forms of poetry for corrupting the character would seem to give little comfort to later writers eager to draw distinctions between the confusion of live performance and the calm rationality of reading. Not only is Homer included in the indictment, but references to the visual, so important earlier in the discussion, virtually dis-appear in this final section. Socrates speaks of *listening* to the weeping hero or the chanting chorus; he credits the poet, not the actor, with the ability to move our feelings. Although he has begun his discussion of the theatrical experience by speak-ing of bent sticks, scene-painting, and conjuring tricks, Plato drops his emphasis on the visual dimensions of performance once he reaches the goal toward which his whole argument has pointed, the expression of his moral indignation at the the-atre. His omission of further references to the visual may signal his awareness that his argument rests on a reductive notion of mimesis as visual copying, which in turn enables two question-able analogies—one between painting and drama as imperfect imitations, the other between the natural limits of our vision and the supposed weakness of our moral character.

Despite the problems I have sought to expose in his argu-ment, Plato's ideas, repeated and varied by many later think-ers, have decisively shaped the way we think about the arts. When Hamlet tells the actors that "the purpose of Playing . . . was and is, to hold, as 'twere the mirror up to nature," he is ironically repeating a tired cliché, but a cliché with a long and powerful life. Corneille, in his prefaces, worries about minute deviations from verisimilitude, holding himself responsible to a standard of literal realism for which Plato is ultimately responsible. Similar anxieties about realism have haunted novelists and film directors, who know that some critics will always object to any departure from so-called reality. And when modern literary scholars, such as those embracing "cultural materialism," approach imaginative works with the sole purpose of extracting from them a realistic picture of social conditions and abuses of the past, they too engage in a narrowly mimetic kind of thinking. If we could restore to *mimesis* its original and lively sense of "enactment," "impersonation," or "performance"—and especially its dimensions of rhythm and gesture—we might liberate ourselves and our criticism from a fixation on the exact replication of nature or life. As any actor will tell you, the effectiveness of performance depends upon calculated exaggeration, the heightening of some aspect of the character or action that renders it memorable. Responsible criticism ought not to fall into the Platonic trap of faulting performance for the very gestures that make it work.

At first blush, modern classifications of the arts appear to have escaped from Plato's forced analogy between painting and theatre. We tend to separate the visual arts and the performing arts because of their different relations to time: theatrical and musical performances include improvised, unrepeatable gestures and expressions that will never happen in exactly the same way again, while paintings appear to be finished objects, fixed and unchanging until the slow decay of years attacks their materials. Developments in artistic practice, however, have sometimes brought painting closer to performance, making this sharp separation much fuzzier. The works of abstract expressionists, such as the American Action Painters, explicitly and overtly display the physical gestures by which they were made; such canvases are, in effect, the record of a performance. To a practiced eye, many older paintings also retain the traces of physical action; the connoisseur's fascination with brushstrokes betrays a desire to recover the moment when the artist formed (or performed) the work. In performance art, visual artists behave even more like actors, presenting temporary and evanescent expressions rather than making allegedly permanent objects. And the most ubiquitous of modern dramatic experiences, television and the cinema, have resources for visual illusion beyond anything dreamed of in earlier scene-painting. Moreover, the link between visual stimuli and moral danger, the real point toward which Plato's argument points, appears in a wide range of modern attacks on the arts: those most commonly singled out as obscene or immoral in the recent controversies about the National Endowment for the Arts were photographers, filmmakers, and presenters of performance art. In the readiness of congressmen and would-be censors to lump these kinds of art-making together, we may detect the stubborn resilience of Platonic ideas.

If academics are philosophically reluctant to classify painting as a performing art, the organizational schemes of the modern university nonetheless treat the visual and performing arts quite similarly: programs in theatre and studio art typically lack the prestige of programs in history and literature. Our reluctance to treat the kinds of knowledge taught and gained through practicing the visual and performing arts with the respect accorded the kinds of knowledge acquired through reading and writing reflects another Platonic prejudice, the preference for the verbal. In the *Timaeus,* where Plato treats the sense of sight with more respect than in the *Republic,* he calls it "the source of the greatest benefit to us," a source from which "we have derived philosophy." Yet even in that passage, he moves with astonishing rapidity from sight to words: "For had we never *seen* the stars and the sun and the heaven," he continues, "none of the *words* which we have spoken about the universe would ever have been uttered."[4] In this account, sight is useful to the extent that it prompts words; it is an earlier, more primitive stage in the development of a philosophy that will ultimately be conducted in words. In a culture shaped by that kind of philosophy, visual artists will struggle for respect, as will actors, for whom dialogue is only one of many expressive dimensions. As we saw in considering the similar history of Western prejudices about music, Plato's many heirs have tended to construct a crude binary distinction between words and all other modes of expression. For those already assuming the superiority of words, it has been quite convenient to equate the alleged illusions of painting and drama, to raise doubts about our ability to withstand the seductive power of glittering visions, and to constrict *mimesis* by defining it as mere imitation.

§

For someone urging closer relations between the humanities and performance, it is a pleasure to turn from the unfair indictment of painting and drama in Plato's *Republic* to the much larger and more inclusive view of visual and theatrical experience in Aristotle's *Poetics*. Aristotle had evidently watched children playing and realized how much they learn by enacting or imitating adult life. (I translate this next sentence using *performance* as a rendering of *mimesis*.) "Performing is innate in humans from childhood (and in that way they differ from other animals in that they are the most performative, and their first knowledge is created through performing); taking pleasure in all forms of performance is also innate."[5] In this account, the origins of the theatre are entirely natural, as is the pleasure we take in performance. Crucially for our purposes, Aristotle also recognizes the educational power of performance. As I shall argue throughout this book, it is not only "first knowledge" or the knowledge of young children that is "created through performing." Effective teaching will always have a performative dimension and will encourage a wide range of performative expression in students of all ages. A narrowly analytical, wholly word-based education, by contrast, deprives students and teachers of the opportunity to learn by performing and encourages a Platonic detachment from music, rhythm, gesture, and spectacle.

When he lists the components of tragedy, Aristotle explains that theatrical mimesis is a matter of actions and accordingly lists "the ordering of the spectacles," the music, and the poetic style as the means by which the mimesis is made, before moving on to the elements that interest him more: plot, characters, and thought. He will devote most of his treatise to classifying the various kinds of plot, but when emphasizing the importance of plot, he makes an analogy to painting over which we should pause for a moment: "The origin and as it were the soul of tragedy is plot; character comes second. It is quite similar to the case of painting, for if someone poured on the most beautiful colors without order, he would not please us as much as if he made a chalk sketch" (1450a–b). Unlike Plato's sly analogy to painting in the *Republic*, Aristotle's is a plausible comparison of technique: as ancient painters first created an outline, then applied appropriate colors, Aristotle's ideal playwright will first construct a plot, then dramatize it through spectacle, music, and style.

Plato measures both arts against a narrow and limited standard of realism, then leaps to a sneering condemnation of their effects on viewers. Aristotle carefully observes the techniques of painter and poet without prejudice, and his range of knowledge suggests close attention to the techniques of both kinds of artists: in other treatises, he discusses the mixing of colors in a well-informed way, and in the *Poetics*, he illustrates the discussion of plot with examples drawn from an impressive number of plays. Our faith in Aristotle's fairness and good sense is rewarded in the conclusion of the *Poetics*, when he makes a careful distinction between epic and dramatic poetry (which Plato had loosely lumped together) and gives the preference to drama. He concedes that "we can recognize what kind of thing a tragedy is by reading it" but insists that "music and spectacles, which are of no small importance," are elements that "most distinctly produce pleasure" (1462a). Aristotle's frank and generous acknowledgment of the importance of musical and visual pleasure makes him not only unlike Plato, his older contemporary and teacher, but unlike Dryden, some two thousand years later, who was still convinced that reading a play was better than seeing it, and who dismissed theatrical spectacle as a misleading, glittering disguise for "trashy stuff."

Aristotle does issue one caution against excessive reliance on spectacle, explaining that "the fearsome and the piteous may arise from the spectacle, but they may also arise from the construction of the incidents itself, and this way is prior and belongs to the better poet. For the plot ought to be constructed so that, even without seeing the incidents arise, those who hear them will shudder and [feel] pity because of what happens, these indeed being what one would suffer upon hearing the plot of the *Oedipus*. To render this through spectacle is more inartistic and needs the office of the *choregos*"[6] (the patron who paid the expenses of the performance). Even here, however, we do not sense a hostility to the visual aspects of theatre comparable to Plato's, merely a sense that using a horrible vision to induce emotion is less effective than building up emotion through a suspenseful plot. One shudders to think what either Plato or Aristotle might have said about the public shows of the late Roman empire—performances involving neither text nor illusion, in which wild animals fought each other or tore human beings apart.

§

The Christians, who were often the victims of those grisly performances, had many reasons for disapproving of the theatre. Roman spectacles were cruel, and the Hebrew traditions inherited by the early Church included prohibitions against graven images that must often have seemed applicable to some of the visual representations of pagan culture. At a more basic level, medieval theologians believed that all things seen in this world were distorted and fallen, distant echoes of things unseen above, and this strong emphasis on the short and transitory nature of our time on earth contributed to a prejudice against visual display as ephemeral. Because Christians believed the Word was sacred and eternal, it now became possible to draw a distinction between the lasting word and the vanishing picture—a discrimination still operative in Dryden's assertion that being read in the future is a "more lasting and . . . nobler Design" than pleasing the audience with a performance in the present.

Many aspects of Plato's attack on the theatre were thus congenial to the Church fathers, who shared his unease about the moral effects of plays. Augustine's account of his own youthful love for the stage sounds like Plato with overtones of St. Paul. "I was much attracted to the theatre," he confesses, "because the plays reflected my own unhappy plight and were tinder to my fire. Why is it that men enjoy feeling sad at the sight of tragedy and suffering on the stage, although they would be most unhappy if they had to endure the same fate themselves?" (*Confessions* III, 2; 55–56). As we have seen, Plato posed the same question and regarded the sympathy that members of the audience felt for characters in a play as likely to weaken their ability to bear real suffering with manly restraint. Christianity, by contrast, requires intense sympathy for the sufferings of others, so Augustine ties himself into rhetorical knots to draw a distinction between the improper sympathy he once felt for characters in the theatre and the sympathy a Christian should feel for unfortunate people in real life:

> I am not nowadays insensible to pity. But in those days I used to share the joy of stage lovers and their sinful pleasure in each other even though it was all done in make-believe for the sake of entertainment; and when they parted, pity of a sort led me to share their grief. I enjoyed both these emotions equally. But now I feel more pity for a man who is happy in his sins than for one who has to endure the ordeal of forgoing some harmful pleasure or being deprived of some enjoyment that was really an affliction. Of the two, this sort of pity is certainly the more genuine, but the sorrow which it causes is not a source of pleasure. (56–57)

The nice distinctions may now seem obscure and fussy, but the obsessive repetitions betray the real topic: "sinful pleasure . . . some harmful pleasure . . . happy in his sin . . . enjoyment that was really an affliction." As in the case of music, Augustine can hardly mention pleasure without linking it to sin, most often imagined as sexual sin. The chapter in which he confesses to his youthful fondness for the theatre also recounts the young Augustine's initiation into "the filth of lewdness," from which he cannot seem to separate even the refined pleasures of tragedy. He understands the importance of skillful acting, observing that if "human agony . . . is acted so badly that the audience is not moved to sorrow, they leave the theatre in a disgruntled and critical mood; whereas, if they are made to feel pain, they stay to the end watching happily." And he suggests that we feel sympathy in the theatre "because friendly feelings well up in us like the waters of a spring." But that positive and promising image immediately turns into something frightening: "What course do these waters follow? Where do they flow? Why do they trickle away to join that stream of boiling pitch, the hideous flood of lust?" (56). For Augustine as for too many of his Christian heirs, no pleasure can ever be far removed from lust; the metaphor of "boiling pitch" equates the passions of the stage with the tortures of the arena. This narrow and prurient view of performance, often involving explicit misogyny, is an unfortunate tradition linking Augustine, the English Puritans, and Senator Jesse Helms. If we wish to oppose that view, we should embrace Aristotle's more sensible assertion that the pleasure humans take in being performers and enjoying performances is natural and innate.

We should also emphasize his recognition that performing is a way of learning, a truth acknowledged in the later Middle Ages. Despite the antitheatrical sentiments articulated by Augustine and many of the other Fathers, the medieval Church later found that it needed drama for didactic purposes. Just as Augustine, with his guilty conscience about musical pleasure, came down in favor of allowing hymns because of their usefulness in winning converts, so later medieval clerics, aware that an overwhelming majority of lay Christians were illiterate, turned to religious plays to teach both biblical narrative and Christian doctrine to the people. The *quem quaeritis* trope, in which priests acted out the story of the Resurrection on Easter Sunday, was drama at a bare minimum, but it pointed toward such full-fledged works as the Beauvais *Play of Daniel* and the English mystery cycles. Colorful villains—Herod, Pilate, Satan—

soon provided opportunities for the display of acting skill; they were, in Dryden's later phrase, "bad enough to please." Music was also an important component: there were sung versions of the Easter drama, and the *Play of Daniel* was virtually an opera. Rivalry between the craft guilds mounting mystery plays led to more elaborate sets and costumes, and thus to a revival of spectacle. The clerics who permitted the first enactments of biblical stories probably did not imagine that this decision would lead to the practices Chaucer portrays in the character Absolon in *The Miller's Tale*, who attracts the attention of the local women by taking the part of Herod, playing several instruments, and singing in a "loud quynyble"—a high but powerful falsetto. Yet we owe the colorful richness of medieval drama to their decision to enlist performance in dramatizing the Word.

Medieval visual art—whether on the grand scale of the Gothic cathedral or the tiny scale of the illuminated manuscript—also has didactic origins, though we must often apply the obsessive medieval habit of allegory to grasp the lesson behind the picture. If they were always conscious of an allegorical dimension, the makers of these artifacts were surely also interested in creating things of beauty and displaying their skill. In the twelfth century, Abbot Suger installed a splendid pair of bronze doors in the church of St. Denis. On the doors he placed a poetic inscription urging the viewer to

> marvel not at the gold and the expense, but at the
> workmanship;
> The work is nobly luminous, but because it is nobly
> luminous
> It will illuminate minds that they may travel through
> true lights
> To the True Light where Christ is the True Door.[7]

Suger would not have felt it necessary to warn viewers against marveling at the materials and the cost had he not known they would do so, but his caution against responding merely to the glittering metal has none of Plato's sneering hostility toward visual pleasure. By gently directing the viewers' attention to the workmanship, Suger was implying an analogy between the creative skills of the artisans who wrought the doors and the Creation itself; by applying the New Testament allegory of Christ as the True Door, he was placing the doors in a proper relation to faith.

This medieval habit of reading earthly things as allegorical models leading to eternal truths, lower *types* pointing to higher realities, was inclusive and accepting. Allegory allowed medieval thinkers to escape from Plato's narrowly mimetic notion of the arts and to avoid Augustine's guilty equation linking aesthetic and sexual pleasure. Medieval artists, poets, and dramatists typically treated sexual love as a lower version of the higher love of Christ for his Church and God for his Creation, not as a vicious, secret, or taboo activity. The secular and the sacred, the flesh and the spirit thus became versions of each other. Medieval mystery plays exemplify this inclusiveness. In the *Second Shepherds' Play*, for example, realistic portrayals of domestic discord, sheep stealing, and blanket tossing eventually lead to a touching version of the Nativity. For medieval minds, the anachronism that places English shepherds at the manger is not a failure of mimesis but an expression of the higher truth that all times are one in God's eternal view. In that mystical context, the willingness of medieval artists to regard their visual creations as ephemeral is not inconsistent with their willingness to spend centuries erecting cathedrals. The belief in the eternity of the Word is not inconsistent with the painstaking decoration of medieval manuscripts by *illuminations* (a wonderful word for pictures), which bring the visual and the verbal together in compelling combinations.

§

The dramatic recovery and rapid dissemination of ancient knowledge that we call the Renaissance altered theory and practice once more. Most of the surviving ancient knowledge was text-based, and the first wave of Renaissance scholarly activity was textual work: editing, translation, commentary, publication in print. Greek and Latin plays unknown to medieval readers were among the works recovered; the influence of such ancient dramatists as Seneca was a significant factor in the emergence of secular Renaissance drama, and the discovery that much of the ancient Greek drama had been sung provided an impulse for the invention of opera. The visual arts, however, lost prestige in Renaissance theory. Classical lists of the Muses included goddesses supporting eloquence, music, dance, and several kinds of poetry, but no muse of painting; the fabled works of the Greek painter Apelles and other ancient artists had long since vanished. Poets, by contrast, could proudly invoke their muses and could turn to Homer and Virgil as models for imitation and sources of authority. Even music could claim higher status, despite the disappearance of most ancient musical notation, because the Pythagorean theory of music held an honorable place in the medieval scheme of education, and music was therefore counted among the seven liberal arts. There was no equivalent place in education for the visual arts, and the low prestige of working with one's hands led to a classification of painting and especially sculpture as mechanical skills rather than liberal arts.

Significantly, this intellectual downgrading of the visual arts occurred just as Renaissance painters were achieving such stunning improvements in technique as the invention of perspective. The analogous insistence that music must be subordinate to words occurred just as composers were achieving similar improvements in harmonic and contrapuntal complexity. In both cases, Renaissance *literati* claimed to be applying the principles of the ancients, but in both cases it is easy to detect their nervousness about the expressive power the nonverbal arts were developing in their own time. Fascinated by words and convinced of the persuasive, even moral power of rhetoric, Renaissance scholars sought to deny the existence of such expressive powers in the other arts. The revival of Platonism in the Renaissance provided authority for such prejudices. Some of the attitudes I am deploring in modern humanities scholars originate with the learned Renaissance humanists, who were often more hostile to the arts than their allegedly narrow, ignorant, and superstitious medieval forbears.

Some Renaissance painters recognized the unfairness of these attitudes. Leonardo da Vinci, in a treatise comparing painting to the other arts, wittily turns the charge of ignorance against the "scribes," pointing to the crippling limits of a knowledge based only on words: "As the scribes have had no knowledge of the science of painting they could not assign to it its rightful place or share; and painting does not display her accomplishment in words; therefore she was classed below the sciences, through ignorance—but she does not thereby lose any of her divine quality."[8] The personification of painting here as female and divine amounts to the invention of a Muse; Leonardo is imagining an alternate mythology in which painting, though mute, "display[s] her accomplishment" in a performative mode. For Giovanni Paulo Lomazzo, writing later in the sixteenth century, painting is "the *Counterfeiter* and (as it were) the very *Ape* of Nature: whose quantity, eminencie, and colours, it ever striveth to imitate, performing the same by the helpe of *Geometry, Arithmeticke, Perspective,* and *Naturall Philosophie,* with most infallible demonstrations."[9] By claiming that painters use geometry and arithmetic, which were among the seven liberal arts of medieval education, Lomazzo hopes to draw painting into their orbit; by linking perspective to science and speaking of "infallible demonstrations," he hopes to gain the respect of those interested in the new scientific discoveries of the Renaissance. But by defining painting as "the very *Ape* of Nature . . . performing" the work of imitation, Lomazzo also assimilates the visual to the performative. Putting a reverse spin on the argument of Plato, who had blamed the arousal of improper emotions in the drama on faulty mimesis, he insists that viewers encountering an exact mimesis will automatically experience corresponding emotions. "A picture artificially expressing the true naturall *motions,*" he tells us, "will (surely) cause the beholder . . . to desire a beautifull young woman for his wife, when he seeth her painted naked." Here the sexual arousal that Augustine had feared as inevitable in the theatre becomes a reason for admiring painting. Shrewdly appropriating a myth about another art, Lomazzo compares the emotional effects of paintings to "those Miracles of the ancient Musitians; who with the variety of their melodious harmony, were wont to stirre men up to wrath and indignation, love, warres, honourable attemptes, and all other affections, as they listed" (II, 1-2).

Another of his examples is the claim that the beholder will "be mooved and waxe furious when he beholdeth a battel most lively described." Renaissance dramatists also sought a lively presentation of famous battles, though they were painfully aware that they risked bathos when they tried to convince their audiences that three soldiers with pasteboard shields constituted an army. Conceding the impossibility of exact imitation, the prologue to Shakespeare's *Henry the Fifth* immediately appeals to the imagination:

O, for a Muse of fire, that would ascend
The brightest heaven of invention:
A kingdom for a stage, princes to act
And monarchs to behold the swelling scene!
Then should the warlike Harry, like himself,
Assume the port of Mars; and at his heels,
Leash'd in like hounds, should famine, sword, and fire
Crouch for employment. But pardon, gentles all,
The flat unraised spirits that hath dar'd
On this unworthy scaffold to bring forth
So great an object: can this cockpit hold
The vasty fields of France? or may we cram
Within this wooden O the very casques
That did affright the air at Agincourt?

(I.i.1–14)

Shakespeare dreams of "a Muse of fire" who could conjure up an authentic "Harry, like himself," with a whole "kingdom for a stage," but his desire for effective theatre transcends mere realism. Ascending to "the brightest heaven of *invention*," the Muse will make possible a poetic enhancement of reality: King Henry will actually look like the god Mars, with "famine, sword, and fire" "leash'd in like hounds" at his side. No technical innovation could transform the "unworthy scaffold" of Shakespeare's limited theatre—a bare stage, a few props, and the light of the open sky—into "the vasty fields of France." His verbal invention and the gestural skill of the actors will have to do that by stimulating the imagination of the audience.

Shakespeare's acute sense of the visual limits of his theatre, most apparent in the reference to the actors as "flat unraised spirits," may reflect the recent success of visual artists in producing the effect of three-dimensional reality. But when the art of perspective was applied to set design, first in elaborate *intermezzi* designed for noble weddings in Italy, then in the splendid scenery produced by Inigo Jones for the Stuart court masques, playwrights were more jealous than grateful. Ben Jonson, who collaborated with Jones on a number of masques, eventually quarreled with his partner over the issue of whose name should appear first on the title page of *Love's Triumph through Callipolis*. Jones's claim that his name should come first was a recognition of how much the success of these performances depended upon brilliant visual illusions—descents from the clouds and miraculous transformations. Jonson's resistance, which led to his being replaced by other poets, was a doomed and stubborn claim that poetry alone could exert lasting moral force, while visual effects must be temporary. "It is a noble and just advantage," he wrote in a preface to an earlier masque, "that the things subjected to *understanding* have of those which are objected to *sense,* that the one sort are but momentarie, and meerely taking; the other impressing, and lasting: Else the glorie of all these *solemnities* had perish'd like a blaze, and gone out, in the *beholders* eyes."[10] Like the candles that lit them, argues Jonson, the scenes must vanish; the words will remain in the printed book. He continues by equating the sensual, visual aspects of the theatre with bodies, the verbal with souls, again by invoking time: "So short-liv'd are the *bodies* of all things, in comparison of their *soules.*"

This argument may strike us as Platonic (and it is), but in Jonson's immediate context, it is also strongly Protestant. John Calvin, using the example of God's speaking from the burning bush, had pointed out that Moses "heard a voice, [he] did not see a body,"[11] and the Protestant emphasis on reading the Bible and preaching the gospel entailed a rejection of the Roman Catholic emphasis on the drama of the liturgy and the power of visual images. English Puritans regarded Archbishop

Laud's program to increase liturgical spectacle in the Church of England as a dangerous innovation, a regression toward the dreaded Papists. Laud described the altar as "the greatest place of God's residence upon earth, . . . greater than the pulpit; for there 'tis *Hoc est corpus meum,* 'This is my body'; but in the pulpit 'tis at most but *Hoc est verbum meum,* 'This is my word.'"[12] His Puritan opponents replied that "the Word preached [was] the meanes to beget men to a new life" and argued that believers dependent on the evidence of their senses were like doubting Thomas, crudely desiring to touch a Savior who had already spoken the words of their salvation.[13]

Ben Jonson was no Puritan. He flirted with Catholicism in his youth and created satirical caricatures of sanctimonious Puritans in his city comedies. Yet in the angry, polemical "Expostulation with Inigo Jones" (1632), he sounds for all the world like an iconoclast, implying that Jones's art is superstitious, fraudulent, and (by extension) Papist:

> But wisest Inigo! who can reflect
> On the new priming of thy old Signe postes,
> Reviving with fresh coulors the pale Ghosts
> Of thy dead Standards: or (with miracle) see
> Thy twice conceyvd, thrice payd for Imagery?
> And not fall downe before it? and confess
> Allmighty Architecture?[14]

Jonson presents the theatre architect as a dealer in bogus miracles, like Spenser's Archimago. Ironically, his appropriation of anti-Catholic rhetoric brings his argument here quite close to those the English Puritans were making against all forms of drama. Nine years later, they would close the theatres.

§

In this atmosphere, with the idea of mimesis under attack in both sacred and secular contexts, no serious seventeenth-century apologist could repeat the thin argument Lomazzo had mounted on behalf of painting just fifty years earlier, that it moved the viewer by its mimetic precision alone. Instead, we find in treatises of this period a willingness to concede that mere representation is insufficient and a new emphasis on imagination and inspiration—qualities that poets had long and jealously guarded as their own. Franciscus Junius, a Flemish scholar who came to England as the curator of the Earl of Arundel's painting collection, made this kind of argument in his influential treatise *The Painting of the Ancients* (1638), moving beyond the "imitation of naturall things" to posit "another sort of imitation, by which . . . the Artificer emboldeneth himselfe to meddle also with such things as doe *not* offer themselves to the eyes of men."[15] In order to make space for this new kind of imitation, Junius makes all the concessions that Lomazzo and others had resisted. "It cannot be denied," he writes, "but that the first beginnings of Art have been very poore and imperfect; . . . they could not much be advanced by a bare Imitation. . . . And . . . these Arts would alwayes have been at a stay, or rather growne worse and worse, if Phantasie had not supplied what Imitation could not performe" (29). In that last phrase, which reads like a summary of Shakespeare's prologue, Junius begins the process of undoing some of the damage done by Plato's shrunken definition of *mimesis*. After centuries in which the discussion of the visual had been imprisoned by a fixation on verisimilitude, this passage takes a crucial first step toward the liberation of the artist by claiming for painters the right to paint what they have not seen.

As Junius goes on to compare poets and painters, his language enacts the passion of invention, and his imagery turns erotic. He speaks of "*Poets* impelled by the sudden heate of a thoroughly stirred Phantasie, . . . [who] cleerely behold the round rings of prettily dancing Nymphs, together with the ambushes of lurking lecherous Satyrs." Like Lomazzo, Junius employs sexual imagery without embarrassment, but in his case the arousal comes not from viewing a lifelike painting but from exercising the imagination. His account of artistic creation, in poets and painters, evokes the imagery of male orgasm:

> Their minds being once in agitation cannot containe themselves any longer, but out it must whatsoever they have conceived; it is not possible for them to rest, untill they have eased their free spirit of such a burden, powring out the fulnesses of their jolly conceits. . . . *Painters* in like manner doe fall to their worke invited and drawne on by the tickling pleasure of their nimble Imaginations; for lighting upon some Poeticall or Historicall argument, sometimes also upon an invention wrought out by their own Phantasie, . . . feeling themselves well filled with a quick and lively imagination of the whole worke, they make haste to ease their overcharged braines by a speedie pourtraying of the conceit. (60–62)

No longer a mere copyist, the painter is now a lusty creator, his work a scattering of potent seed. How wonderful to think of this revolutionary doctrine coming from a scholar, a humanist, a curator! Junius clears away the rubbish of confining theories and claims for working painters the right to exercise their imagination. His choice of a masculine myth of creation, as opposed to the feminine myth of gestation and delivery, is doubtless an answer to centuries of criticism dismissing the nonverbal arts as effeminate.

Other writers on art were quick to adopt and develop these ideas. William Sanderson, in a practical treatise on painting published in 1658, brings fancy and imitation even closer together, expands on the idea of the dream, and attempts to describe the psychology of artistic creation:

> The darkness of night awakes our *Speculations* of the day; when sleep failes, the *Mind* does, then, digest the conceived things into Order. . . . *Fancie* supplyes Imitation's weakness; the property and Office whereof, is to *retain* those images, and figures, which the Common *Sense* receives: First, from the *exterior* sense; and then transmits it to the *judgment;* from thence, to the *fancie;* and there locked up, and covered in the *memory.* . . . Herein appears the marvailous force of *Imagination;* A man sleeps, his Senses are at rest, yet his *Imagination* is at worke; and offers things to him, as if present, and awake.[16]

John Milton had evidently read this account of dream psychology or something like it. Unlike Junius and Sanderson, however, Milton expresses a fear of the imagination, which he associates with darkness, dreams, and women. In *Paradise Lost,* Adam responds to Eve's prophetic and frightening dream with a cautionary speech that juggles many of the terms used by Sanderson:

> But know that in the Soul
> Are many lesser Faculties that serve
> Reason as chief; among these Fancy next
> Her office holds; of all external things,
> Which the five watchful Senses represent,
> She forms Imaginations, Aery shapes,
> Which Reason joining or disjoining, frames
> All what we affirm or what deny, and call
> Our knowledge or opinion; then retires

Into her private Cell when Nature rests.
Oft in her absence mimic Fancy wakes
To imitate her; but misjoining shapes,
Wild work produces oft, and most in dreams,
Ill matching words and deeds long past or late.

(*Paradise Lost*, V, 100-114)

Where Sanderson had rejoiced in "the marvailous force of *Imagination*," Milton (through Adam) warns against its "Wild work." False mimesis, "mimic Fancy," will bring about the Fall by visual illusion, "misjoining shapes" to create false dreams to tempt the susceptible Eve. Yet the poet himself, male and blind, claimed to draw ideas from his dreams, invoking the Muse Urania as his comfort and inspiration and specifically claiming that she came to him in his sleep:

In darkness, and with dangers compast round,
And solitude; yet not alone, while thou
Visit'st my slumbers Nightly, . . .

(*Paradise Lost*, VII, 27-29)

Are we to conclude that Urania dictated only words to the sleeping Milton, protecting him from the dangers of the visual? Or do we detect in these passages the continued belief that the imagination that produces poetry is superior to the imagination that produces the other arts?

A few years before Milton's death, Dryden sought the old poet's permission to rewrite *Paradise Lost* as an opera. Although it was never produced, probably because the required sets would have been too expensive, Dryden's version, *The State of Innocence and the Fall of Man*, is a fascinating document, condensing the entire epic into a rhyming play with musical interludes. In one of his bolder transpositions, Dryden takes much of the lan-

guage from Adam's warning speech and gives it to Lucifer, who
looks at the sleeping Adam and Eve and plots their seduction:

> So, now they lye, secure in love, and steep
> Their sated sences in full draughts of sleep.
> By what sure means can I their bliss invade?
> By violence? No; for they're immortal made.
> Their Reason sleeps; but Mimic fancy wakes,
> Supply's her parts, and wild Idea's takes
> From words and things, ill-sorted, and mis-joyn'd;
> The Anarchie of thought and Chaos of the mind:
> Hence dreams confus'd and various may arise;
> These will I set before the Woman's eyes;
> The weaker she, and made my easier prey;
> Vain shows, and Pomp the softer sex betray.
>
> (Act III, p. 19)

Usurping the role of "Mimic fancy," the tempter plans to make
Eve his prey by means of "dreams confus'd" and alerts the theatre audience to expect those dreams to take the form of "Vain
shows, and Pomp." Sure enough, the next scene is designed
to feature singing and dancing angels, miraculous transformations, and flying on wires. If *The State of Innocence* had been
produced, its most spectacular and entertaining scene would
have been framed as a "Vain Show" designed to betray "the
softer sex."

   With his skeptical views about theatrical effects, Dryden
probably enjoyed the prospect of staging a show against shows,
an opera against operas. His critical view of the visual was not,
however, a purely aesthetic position. The liberation of visual
imagination announced by Junius and codified by Sanderson
and others was a threat to the presumed primacy of poetry
among the arts, not only in terms of moral authority (Milton's

concern), but in terms of prestige and money. In his poem to the royal portrait painter Godfrey Kneller, written late in his career, Dryden returned to the myth of the Fall to express his jealousy of Kneller's financial success:

> Our Arts are Sisters; though not Twins in Birth:
> For Hymns were sung in *Edens* happy Earth,
> By the first Pair; while *Eve* was yet a Saint;
> Before she fell with Pride, and learn'd to paint.
> Forgive th'allusion; 'twas not meant to bite;
> But Satire will have room, where e're I write.
> For oh, the Painter Muse; though last in place,
> Has seiz'd the Blessing first, like Jacob's Race.
>
> ("To Sir Godfrey Kneller," ll. 89–96)

Playful, but not merely playful, Dryden claims primogeniture for poetry. Hymns precede pictures, and the "Painter Muse" is "last in place," not listed among the Muses of antiquity and therefore a belated and illegitimate sister. Although witty and urbane, this passage again employs misogyny: Eve, not Adam, "learn[s] to paint" and, with a pun on the double sense of *paint,* discovers cosmetics. The smooth Jacob, favorite of his mother, deceitfully steals the inheritance belonging to the rough and hairy Esau. Through the politics of gender, Dryden communicates his jealousy: the belated, feminine art of painting is receiving rewards that should belong to the ancient, masculine art of poetry. In the composite art of the theatre, as we have seen, Dryden wants to insist on the primacy of the verbal element, dismissing as mere glitter all those elements Artaud would later describe as "the poetry of the senses."

§

Throughout Europe, famous painters enjoyed unprecedented prestige and financial success during the seventeenth century, and technical extensions of the human eye like the microscope and the telescope contributed to a growing enthusiasm for the visual. Stubborn assertions of the superiority of poetry began to look dated and pointless. Joseph Addison's essays called "The Pleasures of the Imagination," published in 1712, reflect this cultural shift: in these elegant short papers, a literary man develops a visually centered aesthetic, giving far more credit to the sight than his predecessors but salvaging poetry by emphasizing the quasi-visual pleasure readers derive from verbal descriptions. "Our Sight," he begins, "is the most perfect and most delightful of all our Senses," and the themes of perfection and pleasure resonate as the essay continues. "It fills the Mind with the largest Variety of Ideas, converses with its Objects at the greatest Distance, and continues the longest in Action without being tired or satiated with its proper Enjoyments. . . . Our Sight . . . may be considered as a more delicate and diffusive kind of Touch that spreads itself over an infinite Multitude of Bodies." [17] The writing beautifully enacts the pleasure, especially in the image of sight enabling us to touch, in a "delicate and diffusive" way, "an infinite Multitude of Bodies." A few paragraphs later, comparing imagination and intellect, Addison deftly undermines the Platonic preference for the intellect: "The Pleasures of the Imagination . . . are not so gross as those of Sense, nor so refined as those of the Understanding. The last are, indeed, more preferable, because they are founded on some new Knowledge or Improvement in the Mind of Man; yet it must be confest, that those of the Imagination are as great and as transporting as the other. A beautiful Prospect delights the Soul, as much as a Demonstration; and a Description in *Homer* has charmed more Readers than a Chapter in *Aristotle*" (537–38). Although he uses "a Chapter in *Aristotle*" as an example of philosophical writing, less likely to charm readers than the descriptive poetry of Homer, Addison's foregrounding of pleasure actually places him in the line of Aristotle, who was far more ready than Plato to link pleasure and knowledge.

Disarming in its candor, this passage is not only radical for 1712, but well worth considering in the modern university, where many of our methods for training what Addison calls "the understanding" have the effect of disabling the imagination. Even though most instructors consider themselves progressive and worldly, our reluctance to produce, invoke, or discuss pleasure links us (sadly) to Plato and the Puritans, not to the enthusiastic Junius or the genial and entertaining Addison. In a recent book called *The Scandal of Pleasure,* Wendy Steiner describes the paralysis felt by teachers who feel under pressure to offer only cautious, neutral analysis: "What a terrible farce, to stand before a class, impassioned about a work whose political implications one must ignore or deny for fear of appearing to advocate them, whose appeal to desire and passion one must bypass for fear of inciting prurience or justifying rape, and whose aesthetic lineage and form one must downplay or risk appearing a mere aesthete."[18] Professor Steiner accurately indicates several specific pressures felt by modern teachers: we do want to avoid the appearance of partisanship or sexism, and we may avoid speaking of aesthetic form because of our desire to display our awareness of more recent theories. But there is another more basic fear that disables potentially effective teachers: the fear of performing, of acting things out, of exaggerating, of putting on a show. When tempted to express our passionate love for our subjects in a more histrionic way, too many of us are hindered by a modern version of the prejudice against "vain shows" sketched out in this chapter. Although we like to think of ourselves as having moved beyond both the prejudices of the Puritans and the limitations of the Enlightenment, the passage on actors from Rousseau's letter to D'Alembert, opposing the creation of a theatre in Geneva, is still an adequate expression of the disapproval we fear:

> What is the talent of the actor? It is the act of counterfeiting himself, of putting on another character than his own, of appearing different than he is, of becoming passionate in cold blood, of saying what he does not think as naturally as if he really did think it, and, finally of forgetting his own place by dint of taking another's. . . . I beg every sincere man to tell if he does not feel in the depths of his soul that there is something servile and base in this traffic of oneself. You philosophers, who have the pretension of being so far above prejudices, would you not all die of shame if, ignominiously gotten up as kings, you had to take on in the eyes of the public a different role than your own and expose your majesties to the jeers of the populace? [19]

Rousseau was in many respects a remarkable progressive; his ironic choice of kings as the kind of character that philosophers would be most embarrassed to act is a gesture toward Enlightenment notions of democracy. But in his horrified rejection of the actor's craft, he recovers the language of hierarchy. Like a servant dressed in his master's clothes, the actor stands accused of "forgetting his own place"; his trade is "servile and base." Rousseau also participates in Plato's distaste for the public display of emotion, whether real or enacted. Modern academics often affect the dignified and boring stance of the dispassionate intellectual and ridicule others for more performative (and more effective) kinds of teaching; when we do so, we too are clinging to status and hierarchy. A true alliance between the humanities and performance would require us to escape from

Plato, Rousseau, and the fear of embarrassment, embracing instead Artaud's advice to the actor: "To join with the passions by means of their forces, instead of regarding them as pure abstractions, confers a mastery upon the actor which makes him equal to a true healer" (135). We do not often conceive of our teaching as a form of healing. But if we could learn "to join with the passions by means of their forces," to experience and communicate "the pleasures of the imagination," to embrace performance as a way of escaping abstraction, we might begin to close those ancient wounds that have severed the visual from the verbal.

III

The Theorist as Performer

In the first two chapters, I have been especially concerned to expose the profound unease, at times extending to hostility and fear, with which writers and philosophers throughout Western history have regarded forms of expression not couched in words. Attempts to limit or censor the independent development of music, theatre, and art—often based on an unargued belief in the superiority of language—have not succeeded in making notes, gestures, and visual signs subservient to words in the daily practice of the arts, but in intellectual fields, words have enjoyed a long and unchallenged reign.

Historically, the dominance of language and literature in Western education was a part of larger systems of power and privilege. Affluent boys went to school to learn languages, principally Latin, and the knowledge they gained was a mark of their power, including their power over women. As Father Walter J. Ong argues in his bracing essay "Latin Language Study as a Renaissance Puberty Rite," Latin by the early Middle Ages had ceased to be anyone's mother tongue. Women no longer spoke Latin; they spoke the languages that would become French, Provençal, Italian, and Spanish. Latin became a language for privileged males, learned not at home but in school; the corporal punishments by which men beat the knowledge of its grammar into boys became significant rites of initiation.[1] That legacy of pain, privilege, and exclusion is part of our story; we have already noticed how men concerned to preserve the primacy enjoyed by literature put down the other arts by gendering them as female.

Objections to this system were infrequent and typically came from people excluded from privilege and power. The first professional woman writer in English, Aphra Behn, covertly expressed her criticism by appearing to accept conventional notions of the limitations of female creativity: "What in strong manly Verse I would express," she complained, "Turns all to Womannish Tenderness within." A few lines later, however, she gave a substantive reason for those limitations, deploring her "birth, [and] education,"

> And more the scanted Customes of the Nation:
> Permitting not the Female Sex to tread,
> The Mighty Paths of Learned Heroes dead.
> The Godlike *Virgil* and great *Homers* Verse,
> Like Divine Mysteries are conceal'd from us.[2]

The implication is that what society codes as "strong manly Verse" is actually knowledge of Latin and Greek, and that a woman writer granted access to those "Divine Mysteries" might no longer write with "Womannish Tenderness."

Another outsider, Alexander Pope, excluded from public school and university as a Roman Catholic, criticized the education given to the eighteenth-century elite as narrow and stultifying. In a memorable passage from *The Dunciad,* he conjured up the ghost of Richard ("Flogger") Busby—the Westminster schoolmaster who taught Christopher Wren, John Locke, John Dryden, Robert South, and Matthew Prior—to describe a repressive theory of education based entirely on words:

> Since Man from beast by Words is known,
> Words are Man's province, Words we teach alone.
>
> . . . .

Plac'd at the door of Learning, youth to guide,
We never suffer it to stand too wide.
To ask, to guess, to know, as they commence,
As Fancy opens the quick springs of Sense,
We ply the Memory, we load the brain,
Bind rebel Wit, and double chain on chain;
Confine the thought, to exercise the breath;
And keep them in the pale of Words till death.[3]

It is quite remarkable that Pope, who was a fussy and meticulous reviser of his own poetic words, should have perceived so clearly that an education narrowly devoted to words would stifle creativity. Some of his language and imagery may remind us of passages quoted in the earlier chapters. The ghost's fear of the imaginative "Fancy" and the "quick springs of Sense" resembles in spirit and vocabulary those passages in Milton and Dryden about the "mimic Fancy" and the danger of Eve's dreams. The determination to bind "rebel Wit" in chains made of language suggests another reading of the myth of the Sirens, in which the ropes that bind Odysseus to the mast—protecting him from music, passion, and the seduction of women—are braided from words.

For the most part, we no longer flog our students, and we do not subject them to the rote memorization Pope deplored. Although women are still badly underrepresented among senior faculty, their access to education has improved in recent years. But our conception of the humanities remains largely confined to "the pale of Words," or as Nietzsche later called it, "the prison-house of language." The relevant definition of the noun *humanity* in the *Oxford English Dictionary* reflects this restriction: "Learning or literature concerned with human culture: a term including the various branches of polite scholarship, as grammar, rhetoric, poetry, and especially the study of the Latin and Greek classics." With each phrase, this definition shrinks its field of vision, from "human culture," a wonderfully broad and inclusive territory, to "polite scholarship," with a distinct odor of elitism, to "grammar, rhetoric, poetry," particular kinds of literary study, to "the Latin and Greek classics," a pretty small subset of "human culture." If we actually accepted this definition, the only bona fide members of a humanities faculty would be teachers of languages and literatures. Philosophers and historians might sneak in through the back door because "the Latin and Greek classics" include notable works of philosophy and history, but art historians and musicologists would certainly be excluded, as would the creators and performers of the living arts.

Though repeated in the most recent edition, the *OED* definition bears the marks of its date. The modern disciplines we call the humanities were just coming into being in the final decades of the nineteenth century, when the first *OED* was in preparation, and the classics still reigned supreme as the defining curriculum of university study. Much has changed since that time, and the pace of intellectual change has been especially rapid during the past thirty years, which have witnessed the rise of new theories of language, reading, and human consciousness. For those of us pursuing traditional work in the humanities, some of these theories look like *impolite* scholarship; they upset decorum and pose disturbing questions. As Terry Eagleton wittily remarks, "Structuralism is a calculated affront to common sense,"[4] and the practitioners of structuralist and poststructuralist methods have gained considerable notoriety because their assertions so often appear to fly in the face of conventional wisdom. Yet even skeptics, of whom I have long been one, must recognize that the theoretical revolution has played a significant part in the widening of our view of "human culture," which has expanded beyond the classics, beyond rhetoric, grammar, and poetry, beyond so-called high culture, and beyond the West to take on a much broader range of materials. In this chapter, I want to explore how the turn toward theory might help us reconsider the troubled relations between the humanities and performance.

§

Ferdinand de Saussure, the Swiss linguist with whom accounts of modern theory often begin, made a famous and useful distinction between the *signifier* (the set of sounds by which we designate a tree or a horse, for example) and the *signified* (the idea or thing designated by the set of sounds). Saussure insisted that the relationship between the signifier and the signified was arbitrary, that there was nothing about a particular sequence of sounds that made them the only way of designating a particular meaning. The truth of his position should have been obvious from the fact of different languages, but the dream of a more natural or mimetic relationship between sounds and ideas died hard: Mallarmé, longing for an onomatopoetic relation between the two, lamented the fact that the French word for day, *jour*, has a dark, low vowel, while the word for night, *nuit*, has a brighter sound.[5] Decisively rejecting the nostalgic myth of a "natural language," Saussure was prepared to work out the implications of identifying the linkage between sound and thought as arbitrary. He was also a brilliant teacher, and we can glimpse some aspects of his performance in the classroom because we actually know about his ideas from his students. After his untimely death at the age of fifty-six, in 1913, they reconstructed his course from the notes they had made during his lectures. In their preface, they tell us that he "was one of those men who never stand still; his thought evolved in all directions without ever contradicting itself as a result."[6] This tantalizing testimony evokes Saussure as a performer, and one striking feature of the book his students produced is its frequent recourse to diagrams and examples, by which Saussure clarifies and dramatizes his rigorous, unblinking account of the relations between ideas and sounds.

One of his most striking sketches, which I reproduce below, shows two parallel sets of horizontal wavy lines, which represent "the indefinite plane of jumbled ideas and the equally vague plane of sounds" (112). Across those planes Saussure draws a series of straight vertical lines, each marking a conventional linkage between one set of sounds, cut from the sequence of possible sounds, and one idea, cut from the flux of possible ideas. "Language," he explains, "works out its units while taking shape between two shapeless masses. . . . Linguistics . . . works in the borderland where the elements of sound and thought combine; *their combination produces a form, not a substance*" (112–13).

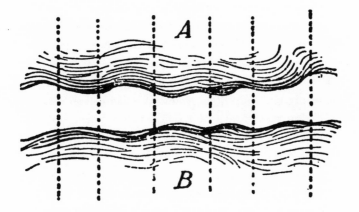

By using diagrams at this and other crucial points in his argument, Saussure enacted the limits of language; by insisting on the contingent, arbitrary, and shifting relationship between the signifier and the signified, he undermined the unexamined and unargued notion that words were substantial. For the traditional belief reflected in Pope's caricature of Busby, in which words are weighty objects that "load the brain," Saussure substituted a larger and more supple theory of language as a system in which signifiers acquire meaning by virtue of their *difference* from other elements or by virtue of being combined with other elements. Thus *dog* has meaning by virtue of its difference from *hog* or *bog*, not because it is intrinsically linked to the animal many of us keep as a pet. Similarly, *dog* acquires meaning when it is placed in a meaningful grammatical sequence: "The dog has dug a hole" or "The car ran over the dog." Puns confirm the arbitrariness of the relationship between the signifier and the signified, as in the wonderful bumper sticker I recently saw: "MY KARMA RAN OVER MY DOGMA." Everything about this joke rests on accidents of language: two words English has borrowed from Sanskrit and Greek happen to have a similar ending; the sounds of the first syllables of those words happen to be identical to the sounds of two common English nouns.

If applied to the history sketched in the first two chapters, Saussure's theory of signification has the potential to undermine the easy equations by which many of the writers I mentioned claimed superiority to practitioners of the other arts. All those metaphors identifying music as liquid and shapeless or dismissing stage effects as glittering and illusory depended upon the idea that words, by contrast, were solid and substantial, dependable iconic equivalents of the ideas they represented. If, as Saussure argued, a word was "a form, not a substance," acquiring its meaning only from difference, writers would have to find another basis for their claims of superiority. Their materials, in his view, were as uncertain and evanescent as those of the other arts.

To his credit, Saussure recognized that there were other sign-systems besides the language of words; unfortunately, he did not spend much time discussing them. The paragraph in which he makes this point, illustrating it with recourse to gesture, is worth considering in some detail:

> One remark in passing: when semiology becomes organized as a science, the question will arise whether or not it properly includes modes of expression based on completely natural signs, such as pantomime. Supposing that the new science welcomes them, its main concern will still be the whole group of systems grounded on the arbitrariness of the sign. (68)

The rhetorical devices here lessen the importance of the subject: Saussure will discuss other sign-systems only "in passing"; he leaves to future scholars the question of whether they will include other systems in their new science; and he predicts that "systems grounded on the arbitrariness of the sign," evidently meaning spoken and written language, will always be the central topics of semiology. There also appears to be a contradiction between the phrase describing gestures as "modes of expression based on completely *natural* signs" and the next example, which underscores the conventional (and thus arbitrary) nature of signification in a language of gesture:

> Every means of expression used in society is based, in principle, on collective behavior or—what amounts to the same thing—on convention. Polite formulas, for instance, though often imbued with a certain natural expressiveness (as in the case of a Chinese who greets his emperor by bowing down to the ground nine times), are nonetheless fixed by rule; it is this rule and not the intrinsic value of the gestures that obliges one to use them. (68)

The unspecified "Chinese" who bows to the emperor is performing a ritual, not seeking some more personal and particular kind of expression. Someone more interested in thinking about performance as a language might have considered a richer example, such as the ballet. There, choreography and convention require particular steps, but the viewer will also focus on the personal and expressive style with which the dancer executes those steps; in this case as in other kinds of performance, "the intrinsic value of the gestures" is at least as important as the rule.

Saussure's lack of interest in such personal and particular expressions in nonverbal sign-systems is consistent with his approach to the language of words. He makes an important distinction between language as a system, which he calls *langue*, and particular acts of speaking, which he calls *parole*. Although acutely aware of the infinite variety of speech-acts, Saussure rigorously restricts linguistics to the study of the larger system: "Linguistic signs," he explains, "are tangible; it is possible to reduce them to conventional written symbols, whereas it would be impossible to provide detailed photographs of acts of speaking [*actes de parole*]; the pronunciation of even the smallest word represents an infinite number of muscular movements that could be identified and put into graphic form only with great difficulty. In language, on the contrary, there is only the sound-image, and the latter can be translated into a fixed visual image" (15). There is some interesting slippage here: in his eagerness to make the distinction between the infinite variety of speech-acts and the more stable relationships that constitute a language-system, Saussure uses words like "tangible" and "fixed," which look like a retreat from his assertion that the sign is "a form, not a substance." At some unconscious level, this passage re-inscribes the very claim that Saussure is famous for exploding, the notion of language as stable and reliable.

Saussure's account of language has the potential to help us think more precisely about other kinds of expression, but the nature of performance will not allow us to ignore parole. Saussure himself, articulating the rules of a verbal language-system, could afford to bracket parole, declaring individual variations of speech irrelevant to the workings of the system, but in the performing arts, the situation is reversed. Conforming to the langue by executing the correct sequence of gestures or playing the correct pitches and rhythms is only a starting point; the performer learns to do those things almost automatically in order to concentrate on expression and interpretation, forms of parole. If we are describing a musical performance, saying that the musician played all the right notes is pretty faint praise; we would more normally want to say something about her *way* of playing those notes, mentioning tone-color, phrasing, articulation, and other expressive features.

In discussing language-systems as structures ordered by patterns of difference, Saussure took a *synchronic* view of linguistics: he was interested in the internal workings of language-systems at any point in history. This was a radical departure from *diachronic* linguistics, the project of the nineteenth century, which had studied how one language developed from another in historical sequence. The distinction between synchronic and diachronic perspectives is also helpful in considering various approaches to performance. A production of Shakespeare on a thrust stage in period costumes respects and attempts to reconstruct the diachronic particularity of Elizabethan drama; a production in modern dress, or relocated to some intervening period, implicitly claims that the play is a synchronic system, whose essential meaning will survive such alterations. Playing Bach on the Moog synthesizer is synchronic; playing Bach on the harpsichord, diachronic. Today, many students of theatre or dance or musical performance practice lean toward the diachronic approach; they are interested in recovering the elusive traces of the parole of a period or even an individual performer. Students of language, by contrast, follow a synchronic model and focus instead on the langue. And here we may notice a historical irony. Saussure was advocating a turn away from historical linguistics in 1913, a time when no European musical performer had the slightest interest in reconstructing earlier kinds of performance practice: by default, the prevailing theory of performance was synchronic. Eighty years later, synchronic theories are strongly influential in most branches of the academic humanities, yet many musical performers feel compelled to take diachronic considerations of historical performance practice into account. The fact that trends have run in opposite directions confirms the unfortunate separation between the humanities and performance that I have been describing.[7]

For Saussure and many of his followers, structure matters more than history, systems matter more than particulars, and the language of words remains the model, even "the ideal," as the conclusion of the paragraph on other sign-systems makes clear:

> Signs that are wholly arbitrary realize better than the others the ideal of the semiological process; that is why language, the most complex and universal of all systems of expression, is also the most characteristic; in this sense linguistics can become the master-pattern for all branches of semiology, although language is only one particular semiological system. (68)

Despite that last cautious phrase, the theories of meaning and signification that have evolved from Saussure's have typically taken language to be a norm. Terry Eagleton's summary reflects the usual view:

The hallmark of the "linguistic revolution" of the twentieth century, from Saussure and Wittgenstein to contemporary literary theory, is the recognition that meaning is not simply something "expressed" or "reflected" in language: it is actually *produced* by it. It is not as though we have meanings, or experiences, which we then proceed to cloak with words; we can only have the meanings and experiences because we have a language to have them in.[8]

The perceptions summarized here are useful and important, but they are not as universally applicable as the writer imagines. When a jazz musician improvises a solo, there is not enough time to think about what is happening in words. If the soloist thought about the process in language, the thinking might sound like this: "The next chord is D minor seventh; I just played a scale fragment, so I'll vary that by playing a broken chord here; since the next chord is B-flat, I'll end my D minor arpeggio on A, so that I can make a strong expressive move to B-flat at the start of the next bar. But I don't want to be too straight in the rhythm, so I'll hold that A over the bar line and make a nice dissonance against the piano before I resolve it." By the time all that thinking had taken place, the music would be eight bars ahead. What the jazz musician does is to play in a way that reflects all those considerations *without ever processing them as language.* The musician, in short, *thinks in music.* More generally, I believe that creators and performers of nonverbal art *conceive* their work in terms of melody, line, or gesture, and that the thoughts and feelings they express, to quote Artaud once more, "are beyond the reach of the spoken language."

Writers in earlier periods were reluctant to acknowledge these kinds of expression because of their naive faith in a solid, dependably referential language. The replacement of that notion by a more accurate account of the workings of language has not yet had the effect of making humanities scholars more comfortable with the claim that there are nonverbal forms of thinking and expression.[9] Even Saussure, in describing the wavy lines that represent ideas in his diagram, surmises that "our thought —apart from its expression in words—is only a shapeless and indistinct mass. Philosophers and linguists have always agreed in recognizing that without the help of signs we would be unable to make a clear-cut, consistent distinction between two ideas. Without language, thought is a vague, uncharted nebula" (111-12). Again, we notice some slippage: "words" in the first sentence, "signs" in the second, and "language" in the third seem to be equivalent here, whereas I would argue that Saussure himself has shown us elsewhere that we need signs and the systems of signs called languages to shape our thought, but that *words are not the only category of sign that can so function.* In the metaphors of this account, thought is like the primal chaos in a myth of Creation, "without form and void" until shaped by "its expression in words." Yet some powerful myths of creation have shown other forces functioning to shape chaos: in Genesis, the shaping force is light, the primal stuff of visual expression; in Plato's *Timaeus* and Augustine's *De Musica*, it is music. I shall continue to contend that those materials, like the sounds of speech, can order and express our thoughts and feelings.

§

Scholars in other fields eventually applied Saussure's ideas to their own work. Claude Lévi-Strauss began to diagram kinship patterns as if they were elements of language just after World War II. In an essay entitled "Structural Analysis in Linguistics and Anthropology," he argued that kinship terms—father, mother, uncle, cousin—were like phonemes, the smallest units of spoken language, in "acquiring meaning only if they are integrated into systems"; systems of kinship, on this reading, resemble phonemic systems in being "built by the mind on the level of unconscious thought."[10] By 1955, Lévi-Strauss was engaged in a structural study of myth, applying a Saussurean method that involved "analyzing each myth individually, breaking down its story into the shortest possible sentences, and writing each sentence on an index card."[11] Grouping these cards into related bundles by ignoring the unfolding of the narrative in time, he believed he found "deep structures," underlying patterns of resemblance between apparently disparate stories. This interest in plot elements rather than in style or rhetoric or imagery follows logically from the attempt to treat myth as langue rather than parole. Lévi-Strauss and his followers, the scholars called *structuralists,* produced striking new interpretations of such familiar materials as biblical narrative and Greek myth by subjecting them to a schematic analysis alert to the presence or absence of certain elements, or *mythèmes,* within a given story; examples would include the mysterious birth of the hero, the motif of incest, the slaying of monsters. In his influential work on the myths of South American Indians, Lévi-Strauss worked in a similar way by arranging cultural concepts in sets of binary opposites, in this case "the raw and the cooked, the fresh and the decayed, the moistened and the burned," and so forth, which he believed could be "used as conceptual tools with which to elaborate abstract ideas and combine them in the form of propositions."[12] There is something tremendously seductive about the clarity of binaries, but reducing a lively and particular local story to a set of formulaic elements always involves some simplification and sometimes requires the suppression of inconvenient elements that do not fit the scheme. Later critics have complained that some of the most famous structuralist analyses were achieved by such strategies of suppression.[13]

Among the elements often ignored or suppressed is performance. Many peoples perform their myths: the ancient Greek tragedies and the narrative songs and dances of the Amerindian tribes studied by Lévi-Strauss are examples. But a structuralist mythographer must resolutely ignore the colorful and expressive details of such performances, attending only to the molecular elements of the plot. In a curious way, this practice resembles Dryden's assertion that "a judicious Reader . . . in his Closet" would understand his work better than a theatregoer experiencing "the Lights, the Scenes, the Habits, and above all, the Grace of Action." In both cases, a stripping away of performative elements is supposed to lay bare the structure and thus the truth. But I also believe there is another motive at work in both cases: the desire of the writer to claim for himself the attention often attracted by performance. Dryden wanted the reader to respond to his text with the complete absorption he had noticed theatre audiences giving to the actors. Lévi-Strauss does not even transcribe the songs of his native informants, but he directs the reader's attention to his own performance by structuring the presentation of his findings on the model of Western tonal music. He calls his introduction to *The Raw and the Cooked* an "Overture" and uses as section titles such labels as "Theme and Variations," "Three-Part Inventions," and "Rustic Symphony." Several chapters have epigraphs printed as fragments of musical score.

In speaking of his "search for a middle way between aesthetic perception and the exercise of logical thought," Lévi-Strauss claims to "find inspiration in music." "Certain devices of composition," he claims, "were indispensable to provide the reader from time to time with a feeling of simultaneity, [though] the impression would no doubt remain illusory, since an expository order had to be respected" (14). This self-conscious passage may remind us of the stanza from Spenser that we examined in the first chapter, in which poetic "devices of composition," techniques of repetition and overlap, produce an "illusory . . . feeling of simultaneity," an imitation of polyphonic music. Enthusiastic about undertaking similar devices in his prose, Lévi-Strauss believed that "musical form . . . offered the possibility" for ordering his materials. "Comparison with models such as the sonata, the symphony, the cantata, the prelude, the fugue, etc.," he says, "allowed easy verification of the fact that constructional problems, analogous to those posed by the analysis of myths, had already arisen in music, where solutions had been found for them" (15).

For someone advocating a closer relation between the humanities and performance, this acknowledgment that music operates in ways *unlike* verbal language, that it has different and quite possibly superior ways of ordering its materials, is a welcome departure from past intellectual practice. I may therefore seem ungrateful when I point out some strange features of Lévi-Strauss's invocation of music. In this very "Overture," he interrupts his enthusiastic endorsement of musical models to engage in an extended attack on serial music, the method of composing with tone-rows devised by Arnold Schoenberg in the 1920s (23–26). Because the analytical procedures of Lévi-Strauss are actually much closer to the compositional procedures of Schoenberg than to those of the tonal music he invokes as a model, I believe this attack on serialism is a smoke screen. "My intention," says Lévi-Strauss, "[is] to treat the sequences of each myth, and the myths themselves in respect of their reciprocal interrelations, like the instrumental parts of a musical work and to study them as one studies a symphony" (26). He is thus claiming that the various myths—like the flute part, the viola part, and the trombone part in a tonal symphony—produce a consonant harmony, a coherent whole. But the way in which he actually analyzes the relations between groups of myths has a much closer resemblance to the system of twelve-tone composition. "The connecting thread throughout," says Lévi-Strauss, "will be a myth of the Bororo Indians of central Brazil; this is not because this particular myth is more archaic than others . . . or because I consider it to be simpler or more complete. . . . [T]he key myth is . . . simply a *transformation* . . . of other myths originating either in the same society or in neighboring or remote societies. I could, therefore, have legitimately taken as my starting point any one representative myth of the group" (1-2). When a serial composer devises a twelve-tone row, which is one particular sequence of the twelve chromatic pitches (without repetition), the composer (or anyone else) can immediately derive many other rows from that row; the most common variants are the same series of intervals played backwards, upside-down, or upside-down and backwards. All the melodic and harmonic material in the work comes from the initial row, and once we enter the musical structure derived from the row, any starting place will produce the same set of rows. The resemblance to the procedure described by Lévi-Strauss, who claims to derive an entire system from one arbitrarily chosen myth, is very close.

What prevents Lévi-Strauss from acknowledging that his procedures are like those of serial composers is his need to claim that he is not arbitrarily *creating* a new structure, as Schoenberg bravely acknowledged he was doing, but *describing* a preexisting structure. In order to defend his analysis as the uncovering of something basic, natural, and preexistent, Lévi-Strauss appeals to a nostalgic view of musical meaning. He speaks of "an isomorphism between the mythic system, which is of a linguistic order, and the system of music which, *as we know,* constitutes a language, since we understand it, but whose absolute originality and distinguishing feature with regard to articulate speech is its untranslatability." Citing an impressionistic remark by Baudelaire to the effect that "music arouses similar ideas in different brains," Lévi-Strauss leaps to the assertion that "*music and mythology appeal to mental structures that the different listeners have in common*" (26, emphasis mine). Like other defenders of the "natural" or "innate" hierarchy of Western tonality, Lévi-Strauss imagines that the tonal works he loves, such as the music of Wagner, appeal to some universal world-soul in everyone's brain. Explicitly rejecting the views of modern composers, who had the temerity to point out that the tonal system is but one of many ways to structure a musical grammar, he appeals to "general [musical] structures that serialist doctrine rejects and whose existence it even denies" (26). That a man who had done his fieldwork in non-European cultures could hold such views is astonishing. In suppressing from his work the music of the people he studied and in rejecting the most advanced music of his own culture and period, Lévi-Strauss reminds me of Plato banning the newer, more expressive modes from the Republic.

If Lévi-Strauss was the Plato of the Structuralists, fitting experience into ideal Forms, Roland Barthes was the Aristotle, the intense observer of practice. Even when working in a structuralist mode, Barthes reveals a sympathetic and sustained interest in the details and techniques of performance. In the series of essays called *Mythologies,* written in the mid-1950s, he provided some pioneering examples of structuralist methods applied to actual performances, including wrestling and striptease, forms of performance whose highly ritualized nature made them ideal subjects on which to practice the new method. In his preface to the collection, he calls these essays "a first attempt to analyse semiologically the . . . language of so-called mass-culture," explaining that he "had just read Saussure and as a result acquired the conviction that by treating 'collective representations' as sign-systems, one might hope to go further than the pious show of unmasking them."[14]

In the short essay on wrestling, Barthes treats the motions of the wrestler exactly as Saussure treated verbal signifiers: he classifies them according to their difference from other motions. As *cat* acquires its status as a signifier by virtue of its difference from *bat* or *hat,* the ritualized and excessive motions of the Paris wrestler acquire their status as signifiers by virtue of their difference from the pragmatic motions of the judo combatant:

> The function of the wrestler is not to win; it is to go exactly through the motions which are expected of him. It is said that judo contains a hidden symbolic aspect; even in the midst of efficiency, its gestures are measured, precise but restricted, drawn accurately but by a stroke without volume. Wrestling, on the contrary, offers excessive gestures, exploited to the limit of their meaning. In judo, a man who is down is hardly down at all, he rolls over, he draws back, he eludes defeat, or, if the latter is obvious, he immediately disappears; in wrestling, a man who is down is exaggeratedly so, and completely fills the eyes of the spectators with the intolerable spectacle of his powerlessness. (16)

This is a lovingly detailed account of the excessive signifiers of wrestling, but Barthes will allow himself to analyze those signifiers only as they function in the language-system of wrestling, the langue in Saussure's terms. "Each sign in wrestling," he says, "is . . . endowed with an absolute clarity, since one must always understand everything on the spot" (16-17). His richly detailed account, which names and describes particular wrestlers, their bodies and characteristic styles, nonetheless returns again and again to sweeping claims about the langue of wrestling, which these instances of its parole merely confirm. Thus "wrestling is like a diacritic writing: above the fundamental meaning of his body, the wrestler arranges comments which are episodic but always opportune, and constantly help the reading of the fight by means of gestures, attitudes and mimicry which make the intention utterly obvious" (18).

In their exaggeration and clarity, the gestural signifiers of wrestling remind Barthes of the visual signifiers of a quite different spectacle, ancient Greek tragedy:

> The gesture of the vanquished wrestler signifying to the world a defeat which, far from disguising, he emphasizes and holds like a pause in music, corresponds to the mask of antiquity meant to signify the tragic mode of the spectacle. In wrestling, as on the stage in antiquity, one is not ashamed of one's suffering, one knows how to cry, one has a liking for tears. (16)

The objection one can immediately raise when faced with this last analogy, that it blithely ignores centuries of history and massive cultural difference, is one of the objections most commonly raised against structuralism in general. Based as it was on a *synchronic* view of linguistics, structuralism was doomed (or privileged) to be ahistorical. In the case of Barthes, the rapid flights across history, which in this essay alone lead to comparisons between wrestling and Greek tragedy, wrestling and bullfighting, wrestling and neoclassical French drama, seem playful, though not merely playful. Barthes was not only an observer of performance but a participant: he played the piano obsessively as a boy and continued to play throughout his life; in the late 1930s, while studying French, Latin, and Greek, he helped found a group that performed classical plays; later, he took singing lessons from Charles Panzéra, the leading exponent of French song at the time. Open as they are to intellectual objections based on history, his perceptions of performance are more palpably grounded in experience than those of some other structuralists. His insatiable interest in particularity and detail, in the parole of the performance, is apparent even in these early essays, written under the spell of Saussure, in which he feels compelled to derive large statements about structure from the details he observes. As he moved beyond structuralism, his natural tendency to emphasize particulars took wing. In his last book, *Camera Lucida,* he identified "the only sure thing that was in me" as "a desperate resistance to any reductive system" (8).

§

As we have seen, structuralism as a method is vulnerable to three fairly obvious objections. The first objection, one made with considerable urgency by traditional literary scholars, is that structuralism eliminates from consideration much of what most readers find interesting about specific texts: the personal, playful, and particular elements that make a novel by Dickens different from an airport thriller. In this debate, which is still grinding along, the traditionalists stand accused of harboring outmoded notions of value and defending a fixed canon; the structuralists (and poststructuralists) stand accused of being total relativists, with no notion of value, aesthetic or otherwise. The second objection, also an important one for scholars trained in diachronic methods, concerns structuralism's disregard for history, to which the obvious retort is that traditional history itself is selective, ideological, and teleological, reading the beginning and the middle in terms of the end. The third objection, perhaps the most powerful, is that the structuralists unwittingly invent the structures they claim to find in systems of kinship or related groups of myths or literary narratives. Their method encourages the suppression of "surface elements" (including performative elements), and deciding which elements are merely stylistic and which elements are basic to the structure must involve subjective judgments, which can hardly be disinterested. Even with the best of intentions, an interpreter in search of deep structure will fix on those elements from which a symmetrical and convincing structure can be constructed. The decisions made, and thus the interpretation itself, will not be innocent of ideology. As we have seen, structuralists seeking to answer this objection fall back onto claims of universality that seem mystical, theological, nostalgic.

In the unfolding of recent intellectual history, these commonsense objections have been less significant than the highly philosophical critique articulated by Jacques Derrida in his essay "Structure, Sign, and Play" (1966). Derrida begins with a display of caution. "Perhaps something has occurred in the history of the concept of structure that could be called an 'event,'" he writes, "if this loaded word did not entail a meaning which it is precisely the function of structural—or structuralist—thought to reduce or to suspect."[15] By the end of the essay, the tentative "event" has become "the as yet unnameable which is proclaiming itself and which can do so, as is necessary whenever a birth is in the offing, only under the species of the nonspecies, in the formless, mute, infant, and terrifying form of monstrosity" (293). Between the cautious speculation ("*Perhaps* something has occurred") and the portentous birth announcement comes a closely argued demonstration that structuralist methods do not allow us to escape from the metaphysical problems inherent in verbal language.

In making this argument, Derrida represents what I have been calling a claim of universality as the geometric *center* of a structure, which he first imagines in architectural terms, then as a game:

> Up to the event which I wish to mark out and define, structure—or rather the structurality of

structure— . . . has always been neutralized or reduced . . . by giving it a center. . . . The function
of this center was not only to orient, balance, and
organize the structure—one cannot in fact conceive
of an unorganized structure—but above all to make
sure that the organizing principle of the structure
would limit what we might call the *play* of the
structure. By orienting and organizing the coher-
ence of the system, the center of a structure per-
mits the play of its elements inside the total form.
And even today the notion of a structure lacking
any center represents the unthinkable itself.

Nevertheless, the center also closes off the play
which it opens up and makes possible. . . . The concept of centered structure is in fact the concept of
a play based on a fundamental ground, a play constituted on the basis of a fundamental immobility
and a reassuring certitude, which itself is beyond
the reach of play. (278–79)

Although Derrida is preparing to apply this model to the problems of the nature/culture opposition in anthropology, we may
pause here to note how well his description fits the practice of
music. In tonal music, the idea of a home key functions as a center. Through modulation, a piece may wander to different keys,
but we expect a return to the tonic at the end; although that
return means that "the center closes off the play," tonality com-
forts us with "a reassuring certitude." Non-Western systems of
music, such as the complex system of *ragas* in the music of
northern India, also have their own centers, their own systems
for allowing but limiting play. At decisive moments, the center may change: during Schoenberg's Expressionist period, for
example, when he had abandoned tonality but not yet invented

the twelve-tone system, he found that he had to substitute verbal texts and other nonmusical materials as a center for his structures; his eventual solution to that problem, serial music, sounded to Lévi-Strauss and many others like "a structure lacking any center," but it is in fact a structure with a different center, a game with rules at least as rigorous as those of tonality.

Derrida's "history of the concept of structure" in philosophy records similar substitutions; his list includes "essence, existence, substance, subject, . . . consciousness, God, man, and so forth" (279–80). Different philosophical and religious systems may posit different centers and thus different structures, but there has always been what Derrida calls "an invariable presence" at the center. What causes the rupture, then, is the recognition that the names various philosophical systems have given to the center are *signs,* with all the problems of signification we have been considering. After that, according to Derrida,

> it was necessary to begin thinking that there was no center, that the center could not be thought in the form of a present-being, that the center had no natural site, that it was not a fixed locus but a function, a sort of nonlocus in which an infinite number of sign-substitutions came into play. This was the moment when language invaded the universal problematic, the moment when, in the absence of center or origin, everything became discourse— . . . a system in which the central signified, the original or transcendental signified, is never absolutely present outside a system of differences. The absence of the transcendental signified extends the domain and the play of signification infinitely. (280)

As Saussure had deprived his contemporaries of the comforting but metaphysical notion that words were solid and substantial,

Derrida deprives us of the similarly metaphysical notion that a structure of thought with "consciousness" or "existence" at its center is anchored to something real.

The next move is even more radical. Derrida insists that critiques of metaphysics, including his own, must inevitably employ the concepts of metaphysics, that "we can pronounce not a single destructive proposition which has not already had to slip into the form, the logic, and the implicit postulations of precisely what it seeks to contest" (280–81). And here his example is the same "Overture" to *The Raw and the Cooked* that we have already sampled. To Lévi-Strauss's assertion that he has "sought to transcend the opposition between the sensible and the intelligible by operating from the outset at the level of signs," Derrida offers the devastating response that "the concept of the sign . . . has been determined by this opposition throughout the totality of its history. It has lived only on this opposition and its system" (281). Recalling Saussure confirms his assertion: the signifier is "sensible" (we perceive it with our ears); the signified is "intelligible" (we understand it with our minds); and "linguistics . . . works in the borderland where the elements of sound and thought combine." The fundamental move of the structuralist, "operating . . . at the level of signs," was therefore not an escape from "the opposition between the sensible and the intelligible," but a reinscribing of that opposition at the next level of abstraction. "But we cannot do without the concept of the sign," continues Derrida, "for we cannot give up this metaphysical complicity without also giving up the critique we are directing against this complicity" (281).

To many, this line of argument has seemed like the counsel of despair, leading to nihilism and the absence of meaning. Derrida himself points in that direction with the image of deconstruction as an infant monstrosity—an apocalyptic vision

that might remind us of an earlier poetic prophecy along much
the same lines:

> Things fall apart; the centre cannot hold;
> Mere anarchy is loosed upon the world,
>
> . . . .
>
> And what rough beast, its hour come round at last,
> Slouches towards Bethlehem to be born?[16]

But in other sections of the same essay, the deconstruction of
the center becomes an exhilarating liberation, an opportunity
for play. Derrida speaks not of an absence of signification but
of a surplus: "One cannot determine the center . . . because the
sign which replaces the center, which supplements it, taking
the center's place in its absence—this sign is added, occurs as a
surplus, as a *supplement*" (289). And in all kinds of performance,
such a surplus of signification is precisely what the performer
provides. When I play the flute, what I add to the bare pitches
and rhythms indicated in the score supplements the signs already made by the composer. If I feel great reverence toward
the composer and believe that the original work is the center
of my structure, I may conceive of my performance as merely a
realization, bringing out and clarifying elements already there
in the score; if I am more aggressive, more playful in my performance, I may want my supplement to take the place of the
center, and I may therefore play in a way that directs more attention to my virtuosity, my sound, or my musical ideas than to
the work of the composer. So, too, with the actor, whose every
hesitation of voice and gesture of body is a supplement to the
bare script, but who faces the same tension between conceiving
of performance as faithful interpretation or self-expression.

Like other binaries, this one is false and falsifying. There
can be no faithful interpretation because neither the original

creator's intent nor the meaning of the signs in which the score or play is recorded can be satisfactorily fixed. There can be no pure self-expression, even for the jazz musician improvising on the barest of changes; some fragmentary original is always there to be performed. The performer is always operating without clear rules, playing in a field without a well-defined center. Moreover, performers knew that they were operating in this uncertain and subjective world long before Derrida—indeed, long before Saussure. The history of performance practice in dance, theatre, and music, though we must provisionally reassemble it from fragmentary traces, provides fascinating insights into these problems, and deserves much more study. Living performers, I submit, have a more visceral understanding of this situation than intellectuals, who have much to learn from them.

The whole debate about the "death of the author," for example, marked out in famous essays by Barthes and by Michel Foucault, looks different if we factor in performance. Because the author's language is inevitably a tissue of signifiers with uncertain and shifting signifieds, we are told, the reader must take over, interpreting the text in an active, imaginative fashion. But in many art forms, reading is not a simple transaction between the original creator and the living consumer, with the text as the middle element. In music, dance, drama, opera, the audience experiences a performance, not a text, and that performance, whatever its conception or its artistic principles, has a surplus of signification. If we wish to be the active readers imagined by modern theory, might we not usefully turn to performers to learn how they approach the work of interpretation, in practice and in theory? Among the surprising attitudes we are likely to encounter is great respect and sympathy for the original creators, often extending to a metaphysical feeling of oneness with them. For the working performer, the author is often present as a silent partner, a collaborator, even when the performer is actively reshaping the work.

And here it is a pleasure to turn for an example to one of the last essays completed by Roland Barthes, entitled "Loving Schumann." Not, it will be noted, "Loving the Discourse of Schumann" or "Loving the Author-Function of Schumann." Barthes his argument with a sad but true observation about a social change, a loss of what we might call performative listening. "Throughout the nineteenth century," he reminds us, "playing the piano was a class activity, . . . but general enough to coincide, by and large, with listening to music. I myself began listening to Beethoven's symphonies only by playing them four hands, with a close friend as enthusiastic about them as I was. But nowadays listening to music is dissociated from its practice: many virtuosos, listeners, *en masse:* but as for practitioners, amateurs — very few."[17] This situation, he explains, is especially unfortunate for Schumann, who "lets his music be fully heard only by someone who plays it, even badly":

> I have always been struck by this paradox: that a certain piece of Schumann's delighted me when I played it (approximately), and rather disappointed me when I heard it on records: then it seemed mysteriously impoverished, incomplete. . . . Schumann's music goes much farther than the ear; it goes into the body, into the muscles by the beats of its rhythm, and somehow into the viscera by the voluptuous pleasure of its *melos:* as if on each occasion the piece was written only for one person, the one who plays it; the true Schumannian pianist- *c'est moi.* (295)

By becoming a performer, even a technically limited one, Barthes achieves a fuller, deeper experience with the music than by sitting as a passive listener—and so might we all.

To the obvious query—How might this be applied to literature?—I want to confess that I have always believed that what I do in teaching a poem to a class is quite similar to what I do in performing a sonata for a concert audience. In both cases, I feel a sense of duty to the original creator, coupled with the certain knowledge that I cannot perfectly know that person's intent or perfectly understand the written traces of the work. In both cases my position in culture and history, my knowledge and ignorance of other music, other poetry, undoubtedly affect my interpretation, as do my feelings and ideas. And in both cases, my interpretation is a transaction in which I am the middle party, communicating my enthusiasm and love for the work to others who have not experienced it as often and as deeply as I have. As interpreters, as the guides through whom young people first encounter works of literature, accounts of history, problems in philosophy, humanities teachers are performers. In the intellectual climate in which we live at the end of the twentieth century, our thoughts about how to perform the work of interpretation, scholarship, and teaching cannot escape the frustrations described by Derrida, in which a rigorous critique of metaphysics finds itself trapped by metaphysics, in which the signs we all use to express ourselves prove slippery and unreliable. But as performers in the arts demonstrate every day, the knowledge that we are playing on a decentered field need not leave us paralyzed and unable to function.

It has not paralyzed Derrida, who has gone on to write a vast body of work on a wide range of topics, all of it presumably subject to the problems of meaning worked out in the essay we have been considering. Indeed, one general contribution of the turn toward theory may turn out to be the unabashedly performative stance of many of its leading exponents. For the studied pose of modesty, neutrality, and objectivity often adopted by earlier scholars, which was always a pose, they have substituted a playful, self-conscious presentation of their ideas. Like other performers, they have gained passionate fans and dismissive detractors. Some critics have compared their writing to music, dismissing both as being without meaning. Derrida responds to one such attack with the following caricature: "I-do-not-understand-therefore-it's-irrational-non - analytic - magical - illogical - perverse - seductive - diabolical."[18] We have seen those charges, indeed, some of those words, applied to music, drama, and art in the history sketched in the first two chapters. That the theorists now find themselves suffering kinds of criticism once applied to performers is a sign of something. I leave you to ponder its significance.

IV

Performance and Promises

The humanities and the arts are in trouble. Stories in the newspapers report the increasing reluctance of British businesses to hire university graduates with degrees in humanities or the arts. Responding to similar perceptions, fewer than 10 percent of American college and university students now seek a degree in the humanities. Graduate students emerging from top programs with doctoral degrees face bleak prospects in both countries—indeed, throughout the industrialized world. Very few entry-level teaching posts are available, and many excellent candidates vie for those scarce positions. So, too, in the world of the arts. In Britain, an arts program that did much to promote innovative work between World War II and the 1970s has become the Ministry of National Heritage, and funding for living artists has suffered in consequence. Even the successful "pairing scheme" encouraging corporate contributions to the arts is now in jeopardy. In the United States, we spend more federal dollars on military bands than on the National Endowment for the Arts, and the already minuscule budget for the arts has suffered further reductions in recent years, with some members of Congress calling for its elimination. The National Endowment for the Humanities has seen its budget shrink as well and has eliminated many staff and some programs.

These facts are well known. Yet those of us who still have jobs teaching the humanities tend to deplore our situation by blaming others. The students, we say, are too pragmatic, too narrowly oriented toward technical or commercial careers; the

politicians, we say, are ignorant and bigoted, unable to understand the importance of what we do. Or we complain about our
academic colleagues, gazing with envy at the funds still flow-
ing to scientific and medical research. J. H. Plumb, a historian
I greatly admire, saw all of this clearly enough more than thirty
years ago. In the introduction to a volume called *The Crisis of
the Humanities* (1964), he pointed out that "the rising tide of
scientific and industrial societies, combined with the battering
of two World Wars, [had] shattered the confidence of humanists in their capacity to lead or to instruct." Plumb believed that
his colleagues were "tak[ing] refuge in two desperate courses—
both suicidal. Either they blindly cling to their traditional attitudes and pretend that their function is what it was and that
all will be well so long as change is repelled, or they retreat
into their own private professional world and deny any social
function to their subject."[1] His remarks need surprisingly little
adjustment today. Some older humanities teachers are still engaged in the almost neurotic denial sketched out as the first
alternative, dreaming of an intellectual life untroubled by the
distressing assertions of the theorists and of a professional life
with expanding opportunities for themselves and their students.
Even quantitative historians, who normally exhibit great faith
in statistics, retreat into anecdote when faced with the stark
realities of the academic job market. "It can't be as bad as all
that," says a senior professor, "one of my students got a job."
Most younger humanists embrace the second alternative, the
retreat into a "private professional world," though the lively,
contentious, and polemical nature of that world has made it
possible to conceive of this choice as active engagement rather
than retreat. The relatively unified professional world of which
Plumb was speaking in 1964 has become a much more various
and contested territory, with advocates of some theories and

methods loudly proclaiming the social function of their subjects, though in truth their ideas rarely reach an audience beyond the university walls.

When we compare these scholarly responses to reduced resources and public indifference with the responses of performers facing similar problems, the differences are striking. University teachers, especially those protected by the tenure system, can afford to practice denial as interest shifts away from their areas of expertise, but performers cannot. Popular musicians who wish to be more than "one-hit wonders" must adapt to changes in style and audience taste that now occur with dizzying speed. Stage actors need to make significant adjustments in their technique to appear on television or in the cinema, yet it is a rare actor who will not seek to make such adjustments in order to reach the wider audience available through the electronic media. Even classical musicians, aware of the positive audience response enjoyed by the old instruments movement, have significantly altered their performing style in playing older music—sometimes by changing the actual instruments they use, sometimes by playing modern instruments in a way strongly influenced by the sound of older instruments. In all these cases, the flexibility of performers, their willingness to adjust to the changing demands of audiences, contrasts strongly with the inflexibility of academics. When I attended an international conference on economics and the arts at Salzburg in 1993, at which the evidence of worldwide problems was all too palpable, I was struck by the determination of orchestra managers, film directors, and Eastern European civil servants to find solutions, ways of surviving under circumstances that would drive most academic humanists to bury their heads even more deeply in the sand.

Recognizing the need for a more realistic outlook, even in the comparatively rosy days of 1964, Plumb insisted that the humanities "must change the image they present," and if that was good advice in 1964, it is much more urgent today, when our very survival is at stake. While the image we present has changed, I do not think we have improved our standing. Indeed, I believe that the educated, intelligent, literate public— the people among whom we must seek political and financial support—feel much more estranged from academic work in the humanities now than they did in earlier decades. In 1947, Cleanth Brooks published *The Well-Wrought Urn,* a work regarded by his academic colleagues as controversial, innovative, on the cutting edge. During its long life, that book sold millions of copies in numerous British and American editions; there was a new edition in 1975, almost thirty years after the first, and the American publisher reports selling more than one hundred thousand copies since 1984.[2] I cannot think of a work of literary criticism published since 1975 that is likely to have such a long life or to reach so many nonacademic readers. Similar comparisons might be made in history or even in philosophy, where some of the best work of the 1950s was of interest on both sides of the university wall. The current academic reward system, however, provides no strong incentive for contemporary intellectuals to address a wide audience. Indeed, the emphasis that academic departments place on publication by peer-reviewed journals and university presses is a strong incentive to produce work addressed to a narrow subset of one's academic peers.

Let me illustrate this situation with a somewhat unfair comparison. In 1932, Virginia Woolf wrote an essay on *Robinson Crusoe* as part of her luminous series called *The Common Reader.* In the course of that essay, she became fascinated with Defoe's talent for investing ordinary objects with larger meaning; her example is the pot that Crusoe struggles to make in order to have a way of cooking and storing the grain he grows. Here is part of Woolf's discussion:

Thus Defoe, by reiterating that nothing but a plain earthenware pot stands in the foreground, persuades us to see remote islands and the solitudes of the human soul. By believing fixedly in the solidity of the pot and its earthiness, he has subdued every other element to his design; he has roped the whole universe into harmony. And is there any reason, we ask as we shut the book, why the perspective that a plain earthenware pot exacts should not satisfy us as completely, once we grasp it, as man himself in all his sublimity standing against a background of broken mountains and tumbling oceans with stars flaming in the sky?[3]

Rhetorical and memorable, this writing is highly performative. Woolf is utterly unabashed in her use of metaphor—my favorite is her assertion that Defoe "has roped the whole universe into harmony"—and we might think of her metaphors as the gestures by which one great writer celebrates and performs another, like an actor or musician bringing a score or script to life. She is acutely aware of her audience. The seductive power of the pronoun "we" persuades us that "we" share a perception that is in large measure Woolf's own, and the closing rhetorical question does not leave us much space for disagreement. Like a compelling performer, she ropes us into her world.

In 1988, John Richetti wrote an essay entitled "The Novel and Society: The Case of Daniel Defoe." He, too, was interested in the way the particular comes to stand for the general in Defoe's fictions, but his exposition could hardly be more different from Woolf's. Here is a sample:

The eighteenth-century novel can be said to form part of an emerging social formation, connected at the least as a parallel phenomenon to an increasingly efficient ordering of objects and persons through written documents and records, as the organized totality called the nation-state begins to materialize. Paradoxically, the intensely individualistic ordering drive of novelistic narration can easily turn readers toward the rationalized bureaucratic norms just then beginning to emerge. In eighteenth-century narrative, it can be argued, historically specific individuals begin to emerge with a new clarity and insistence. Such figures are elaborately, pointedly derived from local and particularized social and historical circumstances rather than from the generalized moral essentialism of literary tradition. Implicitly, the novel as a new narrative mode argues for rationalized social arrangements that can respond to the needs of these unique or at least unpredictably individualized characters, who tend to be presented as such rather than as part of a traditional system of predetermined roles and functions in which understanding the repetition of perennial patterns is the key to moral and social knowledge.[4]

Many readers, I submit, are likely to lose track of Professor Richetti's effort to link fiction with history because of the abstract nouns ("formation," "phenomenon," "ordering," "totality," "norms") and the passive verbs ("can be said," "can be argued," "tend to be presented"). These stylistic habits—common in modern academic writing in the humanities—are the antithesis of performance, and the reluctance to perform, the preference for a general, abstract exposition, takes such writing away from the tradition of the humanities by suppressing the human dimension. There are no people here. Neither Defoe nor any named character appears in this substantial extract, nor does Professor Richetti. There is no "I" who speaks, no "we" who understand. The actors, the subjects of the sentences, are historical phenomena—"the eighteenth-century novel," "the organized totality called the nation-state," "the . . . ordering drive of novelistic narration." When people finally appear, they are "historically specific individuals," but Professor Richetti gives no examples, names no names.

Although it apparently satisfies departmental promotion committees, writing like this is unlikely to attract students to classes in the humanities or win economic support for research. If we write this way as humanities scholars, we should acknowledge that our problems with public image, like our dwindling student numbers and our lack of support from governments, are problems of our own making. In this closing chapter, I am going to argue that one solution lies in the forging of new interdisciplinary alliances, not only across the barriers separating the various disciplines that make up the modern humanities, but across the larger barrier separating scholars from performers. If our problems are in some measure the problems of finding an audience, both among students whose interest we hope to attract and among adults whose support we need, we might learn some valuable lessons from performers, who cannot function without an audience.

§

Our failure to address a wider audience is a direct result of academic specialization, and this century has witnessed the relentless division of knowledge into discrete fields of specialization. The barriers separating the disciplines grew higher and thicker in the years after World War II, and despite considerable recent interest in interdisciplinary work, few scholars can manage sustained careers of teaching and publishing across departmental lines. Even within fields, there has been a relentless narrowing by geography, chronology, and ideology. My own field, English literature, was once a home for wide-ranging generalists who taught in all genres and periods, but we now frequently encounter advertisements seeking specialists in "American poetry 1875–1904" or in "Marxist approaches to the Victorian novel." These sample job descriptions (and they are direct quotations) involve different kinds of specialization: one marks out a particular genre, a particular country, and a very small time span as a discrete "field"; the other allows a somewhat longer time span but insists on a specific methodology. The trend to splitting fields into shorter and shorter periods has been steady since the beginning of the century; the defining of jobs by means of theories and methods is more recent.

Let me be quick to acknowledge that both kinds of narrowing have produced intellectual results. We know a great deal more than we once did about many aspects of history, philosophy, literature, art history, and musicology because of patient, specialized research, and there will always be plenty of such research to be done. I have mentioned the history of performance practice as an area that needs attention, and in literature and history, increased interest in the works and lives of women has opened up wonderful opportunities for primary research. So, too, with the multiplying methodologies: new kinds of interpretation, new theories, have marked out a lot of new territory for study and have helped us see familiar territory in striking new ways.

But we pay a heavy price for specialization. Not only does getting yourself identified as "our Dryden man" narrow your range of experience and interest, but scholarship itself can be damaged and falsified by the separation of the disciplines. Let me offer one concrete example. The songs of the *troubadours* and the *trouvères,* a significant early body of Western secular verse, are usually taught in universities by two groups of people who never speak to each other. Faculty in Romance languages who know Provençal and Old French teach the texts, but they almost never know medieval musical notation or, indeed, anything about the music; faculty in musicology teach the music, but they almost never know the languages. This division is even more ludicrous because the troubadours and trouvères were poet-composers; the same person usually wrote both the words and the music. Yet musical scholars solemnly proceed to teach the music as if it were instrumental music driven only by its melodic structure, and literary scholars discuss the figurative language and metrical intricacies of the poetry without paying the slightest attention to the music. In 1987, it was my great privilege to visit a Summer Seminar sponsored by the National Endowment for the Humanities, at which representatives of these two groups got together to learn from each other and bring their common skills to bear on these wonderful works. They did so by having enough humility to become students again: every morning, the language instructors taught the musicologists the vocabulary and grammar of the languages, so that by the end of the summer most were able to read the texts; every afternoon, the musicologists taught the linguists how to read music, then how to read medieval music, then how to sing. In the evening, there was a sing-through of newly learned material, accompanied when appropriate by old instruments. Although I am enthusiastic about every aspect of this program, I want to lay particular stress on the performative dimension, which may have been the key to its success.

In the case of the troubadour repertory, we are talking about a quite specific and finite body of materials, limited by time and place: the twelfth and thirteenth centuries, France and Provençe. In an academy organized by the disciplines, chronology and geography look like attractive alternatives for kinds of organization running at right angles to the norm, plausible ways to bring together scholars with common interests who are artificially separated by the disciplines. Such scholarly conclaves as the Society for Eighteenth-Century Studies and the Asian Society promote interdisciplinary conversations reorganized along those lines, yet disciplinary specialization often prevails in these nominally interdisciplinary organizations: a paper on Mozart opera given at the annual convention of the eighteenth-century society will probably draw an audience consisting almost entirely of musicologists, with one or two historians or literary scholars "sitting in"; a paper on Tamil poetry given at the annual convention of the Asian Society will draw an audience consisting largely of literary scholars. Chronology and geography, potential axes along which interdisciplinary conversations might flow, often turn into further principles of narrowing *within* the disciplines, as in the sad example of those advertisements for teaching jobs. If I go to the annual meeting of the eighteenth-century society but speak only to other experts on eighteenth-century British poetry, my experience there is quite parochial. Yet if I go to the sessions on French history or German painting, I am likely to find that the papers and the discussions assume not only a more detailed knowledge of historical particulars than I possess, but a much more detailed knowledge of secondary and interpretive work, most of it narrowly disciplinary in nature.

Again, the contrast with the practice of performers is instructive. Sir Laurence Olivier was a great success in Shakespearean roles, but he would never have considered confining his career to that kind of work alone. Instead, he eagerly took parts in plays from all periods and many cultures. Sir Roger Norrington has gained widespread admiration for his recordings of Mozart on period instruments; when I recently heard him conducting on the BBC, the work was a symphony by Bruckner. More generally, we might consider the voracity with which modern dance has assimilated gestures, steps, and rhythms from around the world; or, at a more practical level, the multilingual facility of the modern conductor, who is likely to appear in a given season with orchestras on several different continents. Scholars may treat chronology and geography as markers of specialization, but performers resist those kinds of specialization in their eagerness to reach audiences. In the world of performance, versatility is valued; the capacity of a Wynton Marsalis to play his trumpet brilliantly in either jazz or classical music gains admiration. In the world of scholarship, by contrast, versatility is suspect; a scholar who "changes fields" is open to the charge of being less than serious.

The passion for theory apparent among humanities scholars in recent years offers another possible axis for interdisciplinary conversations. The well-known theorists I discussed in the last chapter have had an influence well beyond their disciplinary bases in linguistics, anthropology, and philosophy; indeed, elements of what is too narrowly called literary theory now appear in the speaking and writing of scholars from a wide variety of fields. As I have already indicated, some of the theorists engage in performative kinds of writing and suffer attacks similar to those directed at performers. But if the theorists are like performers, they are like the performers of avant-garde music, working at a very difficult technical level but reaching only a small audience of true believers. Doctors and lawyers and schoolteachers are not, by and large, reading Derrida, any more than they are listening to Milton Babbitt or Brian Ferneyhough. Although it currently provides one of the busiest axes for communication among the disciplines, theory does not look promising as a way for the disciplines to communicate with the general public.

I remember making this point once in a conversation with a senior colleague from the French department, whose own style of writing is densely theoretical. To my contention that the turn toward theory was taking our writing further and further away from the literate public, she replied that lack of understanding had not prevented the public from supporting massive governmental expenditures for nuclear physics. But again, the difference is image: people who certainly do not understand the technical language of science nonetheless believe that scientific research will ultimately benefit society. The icon of the researcher in the white coat, test tube held to the light, evokes a mystical faith. We humanities scholars had better recognize that we have no equivalent icon and thus no equivalent trust from an increasingly skeptical public. Our best hope for improving our image, I shall argue, is to borrow some of the goodwill that performers enjoy by linking our efforts more closely to theirs.

Chronology, geography, and theory have limits as organizing principles for interdisciplinary discourse, but those limits are usually less restrictive than the limitations imposed by the disciplines themselves. And despite the power of the traditional disciplines, many humanities scholars feel strong intellectual urgings toward more synergistic kinds of scholarship. This felt need for dialogue across the disciplines has been the impetus behind a growing movement to found interdisciplinary humanities centers or institutes, which attempt to provide opportunities for highly trained specialists to broaden their perspectives in discourse with their counterparts from other disciplines.

I have just completed eight years as the first director of one such organization, the Institute for the Humanities at the University of Michigan; the Thomas Reid Institute at Aberdeen has many of the same goals. At Michigan, the institute now awards fellowships to seven or eight faculty members and five or six graduate students, who are resident in our space for an entire academic year. To that core group, we add nine or ten Visiting Fellows, typically in residence for about a month each. We organize our annual activities around a theme, carefully choosing themes that do not by definition exclude any particular discipline, country, or period. Would-be fellows apply by describing how their individual research projects connect to the theme; our public programs—a weekly brown-bag lunch with a short paper, a monthly catered lunch with a longer paper, two or three conferences, and a number of arts events—are continuing variations on the theme. This system, of course, requires quite broad themes; ours have included "Translation," "Economies of Art," "Histories of Sexuality," "The Authority of the Past," "Utopian Visions," "The Geography of Identity," "Work and Play," "Emotion," and "Images and the Imaginary." Although very general, such umbrella topics are at least suggestive of some starting points for dialogue, and on good days, as I eavesdropped in the lunchroom, I used to enjoy hearing scholars from one field explaining their work to colleagues from another field. In these conversations, the speaker knows that the listeners are highly intelligent and far from ignorant; competition for fellowships is keen, and the winners include some of our brightest colleagues. But in struggling to define terms and explain procedures taken for granted within their own disciplines, both in informal conversations and in presentations to the weekly fellows' seminar, participants in the institute program find that they need to engage in a different kind of discourse, and the collective gain is enormous. Many fellows have actually learned how to explain some of their most complicated ideas in more ordinary language and thus have become better teachers of undergraduates, better writers of books and articles for the general reader. By listening to the other fellows, they may also begin to see (or to remember) how their own particular knowledge fits into larger cultural, historical, and intellectual patterns.

A recent institute fellow named Fred Bookstein, a polymath with training in statistics and the geography of the human brain, but a worthy participant in a humanities institute for all that, once usefully compared our themes to telephone exchanges. He called them "an infrastructure for intellectual encounter, a gentle artifice linking up . . . separate conversations over the course of a year." The themes, he went on, "embody an intrinsic discipline of interconnection, like . . . a telephone network: a machine, however transient, for permitting otherwise tricky transitions between almost arbitrary foci of attention. Their effect is to throw the lot of us, one year at a time, into a context of joint problem-solving."[5]

Despite the enthusiasm reflected in this comment, institute fellows are still conscious of the ultimate judgments made by the all-powerful departments, and they often fret about the career cost of time devoted to interdisciplinary discourse. When we undertook to review the first five years of the institute, virtually every Michigan faculty member who had spent time there spoke of the tension between the attractions of conversations at the institute, through which fresh and stimulating learning might take place, and the necessity to produce individual, field-based research. Let me quote one especially thoughtful letter, from Elizabeth Anderson, then a junior faculty member in philosophy:

> One of the great advantages of the Humanities Institute Fellowship for me was that I could, as a junior faculty member, come into significant contact with senior faculty from other departments who shared similar research interests. The lively and fruitful interdisciplinary exchange I enjoyed

there revolutionized my ideas about my own projects, setting some of them on an entirely new foot-
ing [and] forcing me to rethink some of the foun-
dational assumptions of my research. I view this as
an intellectual benefit, not a cost. . . . [But] one
cannot expect to get the same volume of writing
done while one is exploring new avenues of inquiry,
[and] the criteria for tenure in the humanities are
overwhelmingly individualistic—that is, they de-
pend upon what products can be credited to the
individual in isolation, not what she has contributed to the intellectual atmosphere or interdisciplinary community, . . . and only marginally what
she has contributed in collaborative published research.[6]

As this sobering testimony suggests, powerful economic, insti-
tutional, and sociological forces still work to limit the growth
of interdisciplinary scholarship. The reward systems by which
universities hire, promote, and remunerate their faculties tend
to measure scholars by their output, as if we were producing
identical commodities. If the British system is not yet quite as
product-oriented as the American, it is moving in that direction, prodded in part by governmental rankings of departments
based on research output. In the American system, which the
British system increasingly resembles, the typical measurement
of productivity in the humanities is the monograph. Too often,
we praise or blame scholars by simply counting their publications, without mentioning the intellectual quality or even the
length of those publications, and if we wish to suggest their
quality, we normally do so by noting the brand name, identifying as automatically excellent titles issued by Oxford, Cambridge, or Harvard University Press, raising our eyebrows if the

label is less prestigious. Aware as we must be that all of us get casually valued by this grossly imprecise standard, most of us will naturally wish to maximize our output. We will therefore prefer to work in a way that produces the maximum number of publications with the minimum amount of labor. Specialization is one obvious strategy. If you have already written one monograph on early Byzantine arches, a second monograph on late Byzantine arches is a lot easier to produce than a work on Dutch genre painting—not to mention a work combining art history with economics or psychology. Taking the time to learn another period or another field from scratch will slow your progress toward a second major publication, and a departure from the field marked out by the first monograph may worry your senior colleagues, however illogical that worry may be. A second monograph on Byzantine arches, by contrast, will solidify your position, qualifying you as the world expert, the person whose work will be cited in all other accounts of Byzantine arches.

The rewards that individual scholars seek—money, tenure, fame, released time—most often flow to people achieving high-quantity production through strategies of specialization. The groups of such scholars called departments have similar collective reasons to support narrow disciplinary research. In the struggle for "slots," for permission from on high to hire new faculty, successful proposals will typically define a crucial field in which the department must gain or maintain a "presence." A proposal to hire a particular brilliant individual who has pursued varying subjects of inquiry is less likely to succeed. No one seems especially struck by the irony that the revolution in the canon has taken place without disturbing the process by which jobs are narrowly defined. New fields of study—women poets of the later seventeenth century, African-American literature, the history of childhood—simply take their place alongside the older fields. Untenured persons hired to fill narrow slots — whether those slots are old subfields or new ones — are committing academic suicide if they admit that their interests have changed, even though younger people might reasonably be expected to be flexible, curious, and willing to extend their range. To return to my opening examples, consider the tragic fate of the person hired to teach "American poetry 1875–1904" who becomes keenly interested in Yeats. In at least some departments, a project reflecting such growth and development will lead to the charge that the person's work is "all over the place." Although the freedom of tenure does include the freedom to change fields, too many scholars are deeply dug in to a specialty by the time they achieve tenure and therefore less likely to change. Moreover, departments tend to pressure even their tenured members to continue doing what they were hired to do. If a department's senior scholar in Renaissance poetry starts to write books about film, the department's reputation in the Renaissance may suffer; if the scholar who normally teaches a history course on nineteenth-century Germany is now more interested in modern Indonesia, the department must either spend money to staff the course in some other way, anger students by failing to offer the course, or (most likely) compel the scholar to continue offering the course. The administrative structure of the modern university puts departments in competition with each other, fighting over scarce resources, and thus reinforces divisions few thoughtful scholars would wish to defend on intellectual grounds.

Many top administrators — deans, provosts, presidents, principals — sense the need for larger, more flexible, more integrative structures to encourage conversation and breadth, but the departmental structure beneath them still tends to promote and preserve specialization. If universities are to give more than lip service to the promotion of interdisciplinary scholarship, they will have to bring about major changes in the reward structures

I have been describing. An enlightened dean at Michigan, despite being trained as an economist, did just that in the case of the Institute for the Humanities, providing not only some limited funding to begin our operation but a license to hunt for endowment. Eight years later, we have an institute running an annual budget of more than $700,000 (£430,000), derived entirely from income on a permanent endowment that now stands at more than $14 million (£8.5 million). By raising that endowment, we have protected ourselves from future funding cuts and assured our continued ability to support faculty and projects that might not have gained support from the old reward structure. Even faculty who do not succeed in winning our fellowships often develop interdisciplinary projects in order to apply and frequently complete those projects on their own or with other kinds of support. A different reward system is thus producing a different kind of scholarship.

§

In raising the endowment, we were helped by challenge grants from several foundations, but the bulk of the money came from individuals, mainly but not exclusively graduates of Michigan, mainly but not exclusively people who had studied the humanities. In bringing these potential supporters into a strong relationship with the institute, we frequently used events involving performance. Alumni, we learned, are far more likely to attend a play, concert, or dance event than a lecture. Our popular Humanities Camp, a weekend in May that gives alumni an opportunity to interact with fellows of the institute, always begins with a performance. One year, one of the graduate student fellows made a new translation of the *Bacchae* of Euripides, trained a student company, and mounted a stunning production. The next day, a faculty member led a discussion of the play. When I speak of forging alliances between the humanities and performance, I am not speaking abstractly. I do not believe we could have secured our endowment without making that alliance.

If the arts can help the humanities, as I have been suggesting, the humanities should help the arts. When the controversy over the allegedly obscene photographs of Robert Mapplethorpe threatened the existence of the National Endowment for the Arts, some supporters of the National Endowment for the Humanities raced to put distance between their enterprise and that of the arts: "We are the sober, reliable scholars," they argued, "not at all like those wild and dangerous artists. Cut their budget if you want, but save ours." This was a craven sellout. When the arts are threatened, their first defenders should be humanities scholars, who are well aware that much of the material we now teach was controversial when it first appeared. An alliance is a two-way street.

The common room at the Institute for the Humanities contains an ongoing exhibit of art by faculty members from the university's School of Art—a graphic example of our determination to include faculty and students from the creative and performing arts in our program. Most other humanities centers are content to support research and encourage dialogue among scholars alone, but in doing so, they underscore the separation between those who create or perform works of art and those who analyze and study such works. This separation is a relatively recent phenomenon: Sir Joshua Reynolds was both a great painter and a powerful theorist of beauty; the leading literary critics of the nineteenth century were such figures as Coleridge and Arnold, both significant practicing poets; the most influential writers on music in the same period were Schumann and Wagner, original and compelling composers. Today, the separation between makers and analysts in these and other fields is virtually complete: we do not ordinarily expect a musicologist or an art historian or a literary scholar to practice the art he or she analyzes, nor do we normally expect a composer, a studio artist, or a poet to contribute to the analytical teaching of an academic department.

We are surely missing a great opportunity here, for scholars and artists have much to learn from each other. As I have already suggested, there are obvious analogies between the interpretive work of an actor or a violinist and the interpretive work of a scholar who writes about music or literature or art: what the performer must do by gesture and intonation and the shaping of a given line, the scholar must do by verbal analysis, yet each person seeks to find and dramatize a way of understanding the primary work of art. So, too, with the potential dialogue between primary creators and intellectual theorists. The people who create the intellectual paradigms by which we try to make sense of the past and the present need powerful skills in metaphor making, skills analogous to those employed by the people who make paintings and string quartets and poems.

Moreover, if we look around us, we will discover that both interpretive and creative artists are our colleagues. The wretched state of public funding for the arts in America and the declining state of such funding in Britain means that the modern university has become a key source of patronage and often a home for the modern artist. In many universities, then, we can begin such a conversation within the resident faculty, and as we seek to enrich that conversation by bringing in visitors for short or long stays, we need to remember to include great creators and performers as well as great analysts. Finding ways to select such people will necessitate more flexibility in our evaluative procedures; finding ways to incorporate them into our discussions will necessitate rethinking some of the unexamined assumptions of those discussions, for example, the fixation on the verbal that we have noticed throughout this book. Regrettably, some scholars will think of artists as intuitive, ill-informed primitives; all the historical forms of unease about performance that we considered in the first two chapters are still operative. Performers, on the other hand, may think of scholars as dusty pedants or dealers in irrelevant abstraction. Yet only by airing such disagreements can we understand our differences and overcome the hostile typecasting that limits the dialogue between us.

In the year it devoted to studying "The Authority of the Past," the Michigan institute mounted a production of John Blow's *Venus and Adonis,* a seventeenth-century English opera. This was a collaboration involving British soloists, an American chorus and orchestra, and scholars from both sides of the Atlantic; we proudly included a sound recording of an excerpt in our annual report. When the report appeared, however, one of the academic fellows circulated a message referring to the recording as "a publicity stunt," though he had no objection to our including a written summary of his own research. Such attitudes gain credibility in a world where most universities accord a very different kind of status to people who devote themselves to making or performing artistic works than to people whose products are published by university presses.

Similar prejudices apply to academics who act like performers. When someone like the English historian Simon Schama succeeds in gaining the attention of the general public, the academic response to his success is likely to be as dismissive as that unfortunate remark about the recording. "Popularizer," the most commonly used term for people blessed with the ability to turn ideas into stories, is usually a sneer. Yet one of my motives for promoting a more fluid and interdisciplinary practice in the humanities is my hope that we may produce more people who can win for the humanities the wider audience we so desperately need. Places like the Thomas Reid Institute and the Michigan Institute for the Humanities can grow and nurture such people, but only if the departments also come to recognize that we all benefit when a humanist becomes a successful performer.

§

In considering the problematic relations between the humanities and performance, I have generally been using the definition of *performance* that appears as **3. c.** in the *Oxford English Dictionary:* "The performing of a play, of music, of gymnastic or conjuring feats, or the like, as a definite act or series of acts done at an appointed place and time; a public exhibition or entertainment." (I cannot resist pointing out that the demeaning example of "conjuring feats," that put-down of performance we noticed in Plato and Dryden, has somehow become part of the *OED* definition.) In considering the resistance to performance, I have touched on definition **3. d.:** "A display of temperament, anger, or exaggerated behaviour; a fuss or 'scene'; a difficult or annoying action or procedure." As we consider the problems faced by modern exponents of the humanities, the first definition of *performance*—"the carrying out of a command, duty, purpose, promise, etc."—becomes relevant. Before we blame all of our difficulties on external forces, we should ask ourselves what kinds of promises we are making, and whether we can carry them out.

Our promises, like our subjects, have a history. One traditional promise made by humanists was the promise of moral improvement, with the humanities functioning as a supplement to religion or (later) as a substitute for religion. The word itself comes into use as part of the historical opposition between *divinity*, the dominant subject in the medieval university, and *humanity*, the secular learning that began to play a larger role in the Renaissance university. The recovered legacy of the ancient world gave scholars an alternate source of authority, a place from which to call into question some of the more crippling aspects of medieval Christian ideology and practice, and ideas derived from humanistic study played an important role in the Reformation. As the authority of the Church waned in the nineteenth century, many eminent Victorians argued that the humanities must now provide a moral center. Even Cardinal Newman, in *The Idea of a University* (1854), gave a thoroughly secular account of the benefits of a liberal education: "a habit of mind is formed which lasts through life, of which the attributes are, freedom, equitableness, calmness, moderation, and wisdom."[7] There is a part of every humanities scholar that wants to believe in this promise, but the World Wars provided some terrifying counterexamples. Participants on both sides who had been blessed with superior educations in the humanities, and who carried the works of Goethe or Shakespeare in their knapsacks, were not thereby prevented from engaging in atrocities. In America, the architects of the Vietnam War included cabinet officers trained in the humanities at the nation's leading colleges and universities. More recently, the world of literary theory was rocked by the revelation that Paul de Man, a leading deconstructionist and a professor of comparative literature at Yale, had written anti-Semitic propaganda for a Belgian journal during the Occupation.

Faced with this bleak evidence, few humanists today are comfortable with promising moral improvement to our students, and perhaps we should not do so. But I hope we will not be persuaded to abandon entirely our claim to address or engage moral issues. In 1970, the Modern Language Association of America held a tumultuous annual meeting, with some members urging the organization to take a stand against the war in Vietnam, others claiming that such political issues were not the proper business of literary scholars. As it happened, the president of the association that year was my teacher Maynard Mack, a man gifted with those virtues of "calmness, moderation, and wisdom" associated by Newman with the liberal arts.

In a remarkable address, he urged his fellow teachers of literature to embrace their high calling. "Though our profession asks no Hippocratic oath," he said, "I think we are committed by the nature of our subject, which is, after all, the lifeblood of all the world's singers and seers, and by the very special bond that the teaching of literature almost inevitably engenders between teacher and student—a bond that at its best requires putting the whole self on the line, naked and frail, with all its embarrassing inadequacies—to three unevadable trusts."[8] Those trusts, which he goes on to describe, are language, literature, and "a world where promises are kept." At the height of the wrenching discord brought on by the Vietnam War, Professor Mack argued that such a world could be "rebuilt" through the exercise of "the moral imagination." He did not endorse the fanciful notion that students would magically acquire wisdom or virtue by mere exposure to the humanities, but he did insist on the moral responsibilities of teachers, who must perform their part by "putting [themselves] on the line, naked and frail, with all [their] embarrassing inadequacies." This is a very special vision of the humanist as performer. I read it as a recognition that expressing our own moral responses to the material we teach requires the kind of self-exposure that performers risk each time they step onto a stage. A flat, neutral, cautious presentation of ourselves is a betrayal of the works and ideas we teach. I have therefore come to believe that performance in teaching, and in interpretive writing, is a moral imperative.

Another traditional promise was gentility, politesse, or more generally, style. The liberal arts of Renaissance education, from which the modern humanities are in part descended, were those "considered 'worthy of a free man,' [as] opposed to [the] servile or mechanical" arts, as we saw in considering the difficulty painters had in seeking to claim a place among the liberal arts. These arts—traditionally grammar, logic, rhetoric, arithmetic, geometry, astrology, and music theory—were considered "suitable to persons of superior social station,"[9] and they were suitable precisely because they had no immediate application to making anything with one's hands. To pursue the liberal arts required leisure; to have leisure required inherited wealth; and if society did not require wealthy men to acquire a trade, it had certain expectations for their behavior. As taught in the Renaissance, grammar, logic, and rhetoric showed wealthy men how to behave. A training in these arts was a training in performance. By learning to express themselves in various languages and styles, students learned to play different roles. School exercises such as giving an extemporaneous speech in the character of a famous general or turning a Horatian ode in a Latin lyric meter into Greek epic verse taught students crucial lessons about the persuasive force of different genres and different forms. The successful student learned to put on languages, genres, and styles as if they were disposable masks; he became what Richard Lanham has called a "rhetorical man":

> Rhetorical man is an actor; his reality public, dramatic. His sense of identity, his self, depends on the reassurance of daily histrionic reenactment. He is thus centered in time and concrete local event. The lowest common denominator of his life is a social situation. He thinks first of winning, of mastering the rules the current game enforces. He assumes a natural agility in changing orientations. He hits the street already street-wise.[10]

These skills were obviously useful in the world described by Castiglione and Machiavelli, but our students no longer sense a need for such skills, and we no longer promise to teach them the capacity for stylistic variation. Indeed, the teaching of rhetoric and composition in American universities, usually in a required first-year course taught by a graduate student, has swung hard in the opposite direction, emphasizing self-expression and sincerity, encouraging a flat, bland, prosaic kind of writing. An assignment requiring the student to take on another voice, such as an imitation or a parody, appears to be unsettling to students and teachers alike. Like other forms of performance, rhetorical agility makes modern humanities scholars uneasy.

Few if any of us would still be comfortable with the idea that we are teaching our students to be genteel. The notion of the liberal arts as a class marker is pretty well defunct. But that does not mean that we should abandon the promise to teach style. I believe we should be giving our students exposure to and practice in many different kinds of writing and speaking. In my experience, the students most capable of learning stylistic variety are those with some experience in performance, and every university-level teacher of the humanities should be a passionate advocate of participatory arts education in the primary schools. Some remarkable recent studies have shown that children regularly exposed to music at the age of four or five build more neural connections in their developing brains — connections that increase their capacity to learn all kinds of cognitive skills. By the time they reach the university, students who have acted in a play are better readers of drama; students who have participated in debate are more sensitive to philosophical argument; students who have attempted creative writing bring that experience to bear in reading poetry and fiction; students whose ears have been sharpened by musical performance hear the sounds of foreign languages and the rhythms of poetry more readily. We need to encourage students at all levels to engage in performance, and we need to overcome our own unease about performance, making our writing less passive and inert, more personal and rhetorical, so that we may teach our students to appreciate and enact a wider range of styles. The teaching of style was once part of a system of class hierarchy we would now deplore, but in today's world it actually holds out the hope of making our students less narrow, less insular, more curious about and sensitive to the lives of others. "To enter another's feelings must have an effect on our own," wrote Plato in a passage on the drama that I quoted in the second chapter, and one good way to enter the feelings of another is to act them out, imitate them, perform them.

A third promise, one we have not been willing to speak out loud for much of our history, but which I have been promoting throughout this book, is the promise of enjoyment or pleasure. "Property that is productive," says Aristotle, "is more useful, but that which has enjoyment for its object is more liberal. By productive I mean that which is a source of income, by enjoyable, that which offers no advantage beyond the use of it."[11] Living as they do in a world in which money has assumed unprecedented importance, our students are concerned to have possessions, and skills, that will yield revenue. Hence the popularity of studies directly tied to the business world. But there is every reason to believe that our students will have more leisure in their adult lives than previous generations, and I believe we ought to point out that an education in the humanities will give them a richer array of options for their leisure hours. We are not training our students to be Renaissance courtiers or Victorian gentlemen, but we should be teaching them to be lifelong readers, intelligent appreciators of the arts, people capable of being thrilled by an idea. In teaching for this end, we will be promising pleasure, and if you have been following the argument of this book, you know all the reasons why we might be uneasy about casting ourselves as purveyors of pleasure. Like Plato, Augustine, Dryden, Rousseau, and the other authorities who have appeared in these chapters, we are ambivalent about pleasure. We do not easily envision ourselves as Sirens, conjurors, dealers in illusion, poor players who strut and fret their hour upon the stage. We like to believe that we are engaged in an enterprise that is not merely entertaining, and we want to lay claim to some form of high seriousness. But surely this is another false binary. What we feel in the presence of a great artistic performance is *serious pleasure,* and that is what we should promise to our students, our readers, our supporters. By performing the work of interpretation in a way that captures the attention of our audiences and communicates our passion for the great works that we are privileged to teach, we will be keeping our promises, performing the sacred task we have chosen, fulfilling our responsibility to the humanities—and thus to humanity.

Notes

Chapter 1.
The Sirens' Song

1. Allan David Bloom, *The Closing of the American Mind* (New York: Simon and Schuster, 1987), 74-75.

2. Homer, *Odyssey* 12.39-46, following the English version given in *Homer: The Odyssey*, trans. Robert Fagles (New York: Viking Penguin, 1996), 272-73. Subsequent passages also follow this translation.

3. The idea of the Sirens as sexually tempting was firmly established in antiquity; Ovid, for example, invokes them in the *Ars Amatoria*, III, 311-20, advising women to use music as a means of seduction.

4. As Richard Leppert has pointed out to me, Max Horkheimer and T. W. Adorno have explored the political implications of this part of the myth: "Just as [Odysseus] cannot yield to the temptation to self-abandonment, so, as proprietor, he finally renounces even participation in labor, and ultimately even its management, whereas his men—despite their closeness to things—cannot enjoy their labor because it is performed under pressure, in desperation, with senses stopped by force. The servant remains enslaved in body and soul; the master regresses." *Dialectic of Enlightenment* (1944), trans. John Cumming (New York: Herder and Herder, 1972), 35.

5. C. M. Bowra, *Primitive Song* (Cleveland: World Publishing, 1962), esp. 275, 29, 61.

6. 12.184-85. For an excellent performance of this and other excerpts from ancient Greek poetry, listen to Stephen G. Daitz, *A Recital of Ancient Greek Poetry* (Guilford, Conn.: Jeffrey Norton, 1978). Here and elsewhere I have transliterated the Greek in the main text. Here is the actual Greek version:

> Δεῦρ' ἄγ' ἰών, πολύαιν' Ὀδυσεῦ, μέγα κῦδος Ἀχαιῶν,
> νῆα κατάστησον, ἵνα νωιτέρην ὄπ' ἀχούσῃς·

7. As readers of the Greek will appreciate, some of these repetitions in-

volve accents (and thus pitches) as well as vowels. The ῦ sound in Δεῦρ᾽, ᾽Οδυσεῦ, and κῦδος has a circumflex on each occurrence.

8. Ezra Pound, "Vers Libre and Arnold Dolmetsch," in *Literary Essays,* ed. T. S. Eliot (Norfolk, Conn.: New Directions, 1954), 437.

9. Euripides, *Orestes,* 338–44. I reproduce the score, transliterated text, and translation from M. L. West, *Ancient Greek Music* (Oxford: Clarendon, 1992), 284. The musical papyrus (Pap. Wien G 2315) gives the first two lines of the excerpt in a different order from that in the usual text. The original Greek, following the text edited by M. L. West (Warminster: Aris & Phillips, 1987), reads as follows:

> ματέρος αἷμα σᾶς, ὅ σ᾽ ἀναβακχεύει;
> κατολοφύρομαι, κατολοφύρομαι.
> ὁ μέγας ὄλβος οὐ μόνιμος ἐν βροτοῖς.
> ἀνὰ δὲ λαῖφος ὥς
>   τις ἀκάτου θοᾶς τινάξας δαίμων
> κατέκλυσεν δεινῶν πόνων ὡς πόντου
> λάβροις ὀλεθρίοισιν ἐν κύμασιν.

For other transcriptions, see Egert Pöhlmann, *Denkmäler Altgriechischer Musik* (Nuremberg: Hans Carl, 1970), 78–79, and Carlo del Grande, "La Metrica Graeca," in *Enciclopedia Classica,* Sezione II, volume V, tomo ii (Turin: Società Editrice Internazionale, 1960), 438–40. There is an effective reconstructed performance by Atrium Musicae, conducted by Gregorio Paniagua, on *Musique de la Grèce Antique,* Harmonia Mundi HM 1015.

10. Giovanni Comotti, *Music in Greek and Roman Culture,* trans. Rosaria V. Munson (Baltimore: Johns Hopkins University Press, 1989), 17–18.

11. Eric Havelock, *The Muse Learns to Write* (New Haven: Yale University Press, 1986), 94.

12. Ibid., 87.

13. Roland Barthes, *Camera Lucida,* trans. Richard Howard (New York: Hill and Wang, 1981), 8.

14. Comotti, *Music in Greek and Roman Culture,* 25.

15. Plato, *Republic* 3.398d. This and subsequent citations follow the English version given in *The Republic of Plato,* trans. Francis MacDonald Cornford (New York: Oxford University Press, 1945), here quoting 86. Subsequent citations will give the traditional paragraph numbering, followed by the page number from Cornford.

16. For the most explicit case of Plato's suspicion of writing, see the *Phaedrus,* esp. 278 a-b.

17. A. Bartlett Giamatti, "On Behalf of the Humanities," in *A Free and Ordered Space* (New York: W. W. Norton, 1988), 138.

18. 10.607c. Here I have preferred the translation of Allan Bloom (New York: Basic Books, 1968), 291, which correctly catches the plural nature of poetry in this passage.

19. Higini Anglès, "Latin Chant Before St. Gregory," in *The New Oxford History of Music*, vol. 2, ed. Dom Anselm Hughes ((London: Oxford University Press, 1954), 68–69; translation mine. Several Ambrosian hymns may be heard on *A Treasury of Early Music. Vol. 1: Music of the Middle Ages* (Haydn Society Records HSE-9100).

20. Augustine, *Confessions*, X, 33, trans. R. S. Pine-Coffin (Middlesex: Penguin, 1961), 238.

21. For a much fuller discussion, with an analysis of a representative sequence by Notker, see Winn, *Unsuspected Eloquence: A History of the Relations between Poetry and Music* (New Haven: Yale University Press, 1981), 59–69.

22. *Salve sancta parens*, from the *Worcester Fragments*, ed. Luther A. Dittmer (Rome: American Institute of Musicology, 1957), no. 64. There is an excellent recording by the Academia Monteverdiana, conducted by Denis Stevens (Nonesuch H-71308).

23. Following the translation by Denis Stevens and Alexander Blachly printed in the liner notes to the Nonesuch recording.

24. For a text and translation, see Gordon Athol Anderson, *The Latin Compositions in Fascicules VII and VIII of the Notre Dame Manuscript Wolfenbüttel Hemlstadt 1099 (1206)* (New York: Institute for Medieval Music, 1968), 1:7–8, 12.

25. Isidore of Seville, *Etymologies*, XI, ii, 30–32.

26. "A Cantata," following the text and music given in *The Poems of Jonathan Swift*, ed. Harold Williams, 3 vols. (Oxford: Clarendon, 1937), 3:956–58. There is, alas, no commercial recording.

27. For a detailed account of Monteverdi's career as a reader and setter of various kinds of poetry, see Gary Tomlinson, *Monteverdi and the End of the Renaissance* (Berkeley: University of California Press, 1987).

28. Edmund Spenser, *The Faerie Queene*, 2.12.64–65. This and all citations of Spenser follow the text given in *Spenser: Poetical Works*, ed. J. C. Smith and E. De Selincourt (London: Oxford University Press, 1970); I have normalized *v* and *u*, *i* and *j*.

29. This and all citations of Milton follow *Complete Poems and Major Prose*, ed. Merritt Y. Hughes (Indianapolis: Bobbs-Merrill, 1957).

30. *OED*, s.v. "pledge," definition 2d.

31. Wherever possible, quotations from Dryden follow *The Works of John Dryden*, ed. Edward Niles Hooker, H. T. Swedenberg, et al. (Berkeley: University of California Press, 1955–), here cited as *Works*. For works not yet published in the California edition, including *King Arthur*, I follow the first London editions, citing by page number.

32. Following the version given in *The Music in King Arthur*, ed. Margaret Laurie (Sevenoaks, Kent: Novello, 1972), omitting editorial realization of the figured bass. There are at least four recordings of *King Arthur* currently available: recent versions on old instruments conducted by John Eliot Gardiner (Erato 2292-45211-2), Trevor Pinnock (Archiv 435490-2), and William Christie (Erato 4509 98535-2), and a less "authentic" but often very musical performance conducted by the late Alfred Deller (Harmonia Mundi HMA 190200 or HMC 90252/53; also available from the Musical Heritage Society 824188A).

33. For a fine account of these developments, see John Neubauer, *The Emancipation of Music from Language* (New Haven: Yale University Press, 1986).

34. M. H. Abrams, *The Mirror and the Lamp* (New York: Oxford University Press, 1953), 50.

35. Kant, *Critique of Judgment*, I, ii, 53, trans. J. H. Bernard (New York: Hafner, 1951), 172.

36. Lawrence Binyon, *The Sirens, An Ode* (London: Macmillan, 1925), 19–20. The passage emphasizes the continued power of the Sirens, even in a modern, secular world:

> But what if it be that fond perfidious Voices
> With different music lure
> Even us who have cast far from us the fables of old?
> If the pride of our quest undo us, and they enchant us
> Simple as those lost mariners, but no longer
> In dream secure?
>
> If not with sorcery of song in a scarlet mouth
> And with eyes of desire
> You ensnare the easy senses and perishing flesh,
> But with spiritual lure you hunger to entice us
> Beyond the borders of knowledge, O evilly enamoured,
> O terrible choir?

37. W. H. Auden, *Collected Poems*, ed. Edward Mendelson (New York: Vintage, 1991), 181.

Chapter 2.
"Vain Shows"

1. Antonin Artaud, *The Theater and Its Double,* trans. Mary Caroline Richards (New York: Grove Press, 1958), 37.

2. Eva C. Keuls, *Plato and Greek Painting* (Leiden: Brill, 1978), 10, emphasis mine.

3. Iris Murdoch, *The Fire and the Sun: Why Plato Banished the Artists* (London: Oxford University Press, 1978), 12.

4. Plato, *Timaeus,* 47a, following the translation of Benjamin Jowett (Indianapolis: Library of Liberal Arts, 1949), 29, emphasis mine.

5. Aristotle, *Poetics,* 1448b, translation mine.

6. 1453b; here I have used the translation given in *Aristotle's Poetics: Translation and Analysis,* Kenneth A. Telford (Chicago: Henry Regnery, 1961), 24–25.

7. Following the translation provided in D. W. Robertson, *A Preface to Chaucer* (Princeton: Princeton University Press, 1962), 76.

8. Leonardo da Vinci, *Paragone; A Comparison of the Arts,* trans. Irma A. Richter (London: Oxford University Press, 1949), 31.

9. Giovanni Paolo Lomazzo, *Trattato del L'Arte de la Pittura* (Milan, 1584), translated by Richard Haydocke as *A Tracte Containing the Artes of Curious Paintinge Carvinge & Buildinge,* two parts in one (Oxford, 1598), 1:14.

10. Preface to *Hymenai* (1606), in *Ben Jonson,* ed. C. H. Herford, Percy Simpson, and Evelyn Simpson, 11 vols. (Oxford: Oxford University Press, 1925–52), 7:209. I have normalized *v* and *u, i* and *j.*

11. John Calvin, *Institutes of the Christian Religion,* book 1, chap. xi, par. 2, following the text edited by John T. McNeill and translated by Ford Lewis Battles, vols. 20–21 of *The Library of Christian Classics* (Philadelphia: Westminster Press, 1960), 20:101.

12. *The Works of Archbishop Laud,* ed. W. Scott and J. Bliss, 7 vols. (Oxford: John Henry Parker, 1847–60), 6:57.

13. For the quoted phrase, see John Dod and Robert Cleaver, *A Godlie Forme of Household Government* (London, 1630), sig. B2v. The passage on Thomas comes from *A Plaine and Familiar Exposition of the Eleventh and Twelfth Chapters of the Proverbes of Salomon* (1607), by the same authors: "It was an indulgence of Christ to *Thomas,* to helpe his faith in his resurrection, by the senses of sight and feeling: but for matters of punishment, and damnation, it is good to go from them, and not to come at them: to heare Gods testimonie, and not to see it fulfilled upon themselues: to

beleeve the trueth of that which is spoken, and not to feele it by their own experience" (134).

14. In Hereford and Simpson, *Ben Jonson*, 8:405–6; I have normalized abbreviations.

15. Franciscus Junius, *The Painting of the Ancients* (London, 1638), 17–18, emphasis mine.

16. William Sanderson, *Graphice. The use of the Pen and Pensil. Or, the Most Excellent Art of Painting* (London, 1658), 33–34.

17. *The Spectator*, ed. Donald F. Bond, 5 vols. (Oxford: Clarendon, 1965), no. 411, vol. 3, p. 536.

18. Wendy Steiner, *The Scandal of Pleasure* (Chicago: University of Chicago Press, 1995), 39.

19. Jean Jacques Rousseau, *Politics and the Arts: Letter to M. D'Alembert on the Theatre,* trans. Allan Bloom (Ithaca: Cornell University Press, 1968), 79–80.

Chapter 3.
The Theorist as Performer

1. First published in *Studies in Philology* 61 (1959): 103–24; a revised version appears in *Rhetoric, Romance, and Technology* (Ithaca: Cornell University Press, 1971), 113–41.

2. Aphra Behn, "To Mr. [Thomas] *Creech* On his Excellent Translation of *Lucretius*" (1683), following the text printed in Behn's *Poems Upon Several Occasions* (1684), 50–52.

3. Alexander Pope, *Dunciad* IV, 149–60, *The Twickenham Edition of the Works of Alexander Pope,* ed. John Butt et al. (Methuen, 1950–67). As I have pointed out in an earlier discussion of Dr. Busby, this caricature is unfair. The real Busby strongly encouraged creativity and poetic "fancy." See *John Dryden and His World* (New Haven: Yale University Press, 1987), 34–57.

4. Terry Eagleton, *Literary Theory: An Introduction* (Oxford: Basil Blackwell, 1983), 96.

5. See his Oxford address, "Music and Literature," trans. Bradford Cook, *Selected Prose Poems, Essays, and Letters* (Baltimore: Johns Hopkins University Press, 1956), 38.

6. *Course in General Linguistics,* ed. Charles Bally and Albert Sechehaye, trans. Wade Baskin (New York: McGraw-Hill, 1966), preface, p. xviii. All citations of Saussure follow this edition.

7. For a fuller exposition of this idea, see my essay "Interpretive Extremes:

The Old Instrument Players and Recent Literary Criticism," *University of Hartford Studies in Literature* 16 (1984): 36-46.

8. Eagleton, *Literary Theory: An Introduction*, 60.

9. This prejudice against nonverbal languages extends beyond scholars. In a review of Douglas C. Baynton, *Forbidden Signs: American Culture and the Campaign Against Sign Language* (Chicago: University of Chicago Press, 1996), Hugh Kenner describes American Sign Language as "a sophisticated language. Using hands and postures and facial expressions, it doesn't mime speech; it mimes meaning. The idea of a direct route to meaning that doesn't pass through some spoken language can be hard to assimilate. Yet it's so." *New York Times Book Review* (26 January 1997): 30.

10. Claude Lévi-Strauss, "Structural Analysis in Linguistics and Anthropology" (1952), reprinted in *Structural Anthropology*, trans. Claire Jacobson and Brooke Grundfest Schoepf (New York: Basic Books, 1963), 31-80, here quoting 34.

11. Claude Lévi-Strauss, "The Structural Study of Myth" (1955), reprinted in *Structural Anthropology*, 206-31, here quoting 211.

12. Claude Lévi-Strauss, *The Raw and the Cooked* (1964), trans. John and Doreen Weightman (New York: Harper Colophon Books, 1975), 1.

13. For a devastating critique of Lévi-Strauss along these lines, see Edmund R. Leach, *Claude Lévi-Strauss* (New York: Viking Press, 1970), 62-86. In an illuminating discussion of Roland Barthes's famous structuralist reading of the episode of Jacob wrestling with the angel in Genesis, "The Struggle with the Angel," Eve Tavor Bannet convincingly demonstrates that "the structuralist reading . . . has been arrived at by *glossing over* [an] abrasion or discontinuity" in the original text. See *Structuralism and the Logic of Dissent: Barthes, Derrida, Foucault, Lacan* (Urbana: University of Illinois Press, 1989), 56-58.

14. Roland Barthes, *Mythologies* (1957), trans. Annette Lavers (New York: Hill and Wang, 1972), 9.

15. Jacques Derrida, "Structure, Sign, and Play in the Discourse of the Human Sciences," in *Writing and Difference*, trans. Alan Bass (Chicago: University of Chicago Press, 1978), 278-93, here quoting 278.

16. W. B. Yeats, "The Second Coming," in *The Collected Works of W. B. Yeats*, ed. Richard J. Finneran and George Mills Harper, vol. 1: *The Poems* (New York: Macmillan, 1989), 187.

17. Roland Barthes, "Loving Schumann," in *The Responsibility of Forms*, trans. Richard Howard (Berkeley: University of California Press, 1991), 293-98, here quoting 294.

18. Jacques Derrida, "Biodegradables: Seven Diary Fragments," trans. Peggy Kamuf, *Critical Inquiry* 15 (1989): 812–71, here quoting 847.

Chapter 4.
Performance and Promises

1. J. H. Plumb, *The Crisis of the Humanities* (Harmondsworth: Penguin, 1964), 7–8.
2. Private communication.
3. Virginia Woolf, *"Robinson Crusoe,"* in *The Second Common Reader* (New York: Harcourt, Brace, 1932), 42–49, here quoting 48–49.
4. John Richetti, "The Novel and Society: The Case of Daniel Defoe," in *The Idea of the Novel in the Eighteenth Century,* ed. Robert W. Uphaus (East Lansing: Colleagues Press, 1988), 47–66, here quoting 49–50.
5. I quote one of Professor Bookstein's sections in James Winn and Fred Bookstein, "The Intellectual Economy of Interdisciplinary Scholarship," *Institute for the Humanities Occasional Paper* no. 1 (1994), 4–5.
6. Quoted in ibid., 6–7.
7. John Newman, *The Idea of a University* (New York: Longmans, Green, 1947), Discourse V. 1, p. 90.
8. Maynard Mack, "To See it Feelingly," *Publications of the Modern Language Association* 86 (1971), reprinted in *Prose and Cons: Monologues on Several Occasions* (New Haven: Privately Printed, 1989), 1–19, here quoting 16.
9. *OED,* s.v. "liberal."
10. Richard Lanham, *The Movites of Eloquence* (New Haven: Yale University Press, 1978), 2.
11. Aristotle, *Rhetoric,* I.5.7 (1361a), trans. John Henry Freese (Cambridge: Harvard University Press, 1926), 51.

Index

Aberdeen, University of, Thomas Reid Institute, 113, 122

Abrams, M. H., *The Mirror and the Lamp*, quoted, 34

Absolon, 54

acting: ancient, 41-42, 44-45; Dryden's suspicion of, 37-38, 86; in Shakespeare, 45, 59; theory and technique, 46-48, 97, 104, 106, 108, 121, 127; Augustine on, 52; medieval, 53-54; Rousseau's suspicion of, 70-71; Artaud's advice on, 71

Addison, Joseph, "The Pleasures of the Imagination," quoted, 68-69

Adorno, T. W. *See* Horkheimer, Max

Aeschylus, 8

alphabet, 9-11, 13

Ambrose, St., "Aeterna Christi munera," quoted, 15

Ambrosian chant, 17

American Action Painters, 46-47

American Society for Eighteenth-Century Studies, 111

Anderson, Elizabeth, quoted, 115-116

Apelles, 56

Aristophanes, 8

Aristotle: 68-69, 89; *Poetics*, 48-50, 53; quoted, 48-50; *Rhetoric*, quoted, 128

Arnold, Matthew, 120

Artaud, Antonin: *The Theater and its Double*, 39-41, 67, 71, 83; quoted, 40, 67, 71, 83

Arundel, Earl of. *See* Howard, Thomas, Second Earl of Arundel

Asian Society, 111

Auden, W. H., "The Composer," quoted, 35-36

Augustine: 19, 24, 35, 55, 58, 128; *Confessions*, 15-17, 51-53; quoted, 15-16, 51-53; *De Musica*, 84

Babbitt, Milton, 112

Bach, Johann Sebastian, 81

ballet, 80

Barthes, Roland: 89, 98; *Camera Lucida*, quoted, 11, 92; *Mythologies*, 89-91, quoted, 90-91; "Loving Schumann," 99-100, quoted, 99

Baudelaire, Charles, quoted, 88-89

Behn, Aphra, "To Mr. *Creech* On his Excellent Translation of *Lucretius*," quoted, 73

Binyon, Lawrence, *The Sirens, An Ode*, quoted, 35, 134*n*36

Bloom, Allan, *The Closing of*